WRITING THEMES
ABOUT LITERATURE

A Guide to Accompany
The Norton Introduction to Literature
   Third Edition / Shorter Third Edition

WRITING THEMES
ABOUT LITERATURE

A Guide to Accompany
The Norton Introduction to Literature
Third Edition / Shorter Third Edition

Jenny N. Sullivan
NORTHERN VIRGINIA COMMUNITY COLLEGE

W·W·NORTON & COMPANY
New York · London

Donald Justice: "Southern Gothic," copyright © 1958 by Donald Justice. Reprinted from *Summer Anniversaries* by permission of Wesleyan University Press. This poem first appeared in *Poetry*.

Wilfred Owen: "Dulce et Decorum Est" from *Collected Poems* by Wilfred Owen. Copyright © Chatto & Windus, Ltd., 1963. Reprinted by permission of New Directions Publishing Corporation, the Owen Estate, and Chatto & Windus, Ltd.

John Stone: "Coming Home" from *The Smell of Matches*, Rutgers University Press, 1972, copyright John Stone, 1979. Reprinted by permission of the author.

Jenny Sullivan: "If Frost Had Written Part of *Hamlet* for Shakespeare" is reprinted with permission of TEACHING ENGLISH in the Two-Year College, in which the poem originally appeared.

FIRST EDITION

Library of Congress Cataloging in Publication Data
Sullivan, Jenny N.
  Writing themes about literature.
  1. English language—Rhetoric.   2. Criticism.
3. Literature—Study and teaching.   4. Norton introduction to literature.   3rd ed.   I. Norton introduction
to literature.   3rd ed.   II. Title.
PE1479.C7S94   1983   808'.0668   83-17449

ISBN 0-393-95350-5

W. W. Norton & Company, Inc.,
  500 Fifth Avenue, New York, N.Y. 10110
W. W. Norton & Company Ltd.,
  37 Great Russell Street, London WC1B 3NU

1 2 3 4 5 6 7 8 9 0

Contents

Foreword

In many colleges the introduction to literature course is a part of the composition sequence, but a part in which little class time seems available for the study of writing techniques. Students and teachers have their hands full with the reading assignments. Even so, students must inevitably write papers in such a course, so writing skills are important to them.

This text is designed to help the student and the teacher to examine critical writing skills and their relationship to specific works in the *Norton Introduction to Literature*, Third Edition and Shorter Third Edition. The first chapter explains the basics of the process of putting together a critical essay, from gathering ideas and developing valid inferences, to incorporating quotations correctly and effectively, to dreaming up a title. The next three chapters discuss the writing of three specific types of critical essays: the interpretive summary, the analysis, and the essay of critical judgment. The final chapter surveys a range of other types of writing assignments, from imitations and parodies to essay examinations. Throughout the book there are exercises to stimulate class discussion and detailed explanations of the writing process with many examples and suggestions to guide the individual student. The material in all chapters can be applied to any of the three genres offered in the text—short fiction, poetry, and drama—with exercises and essay assignments to cover this range.

My thanks to my students, who taught me how to write this book—especially to Pamela Henne and Anne McMorris; to my colleagues and friends Noel Sipple and Judy Riggin; and to my husband Daniel and my family. Thank you also to my editor, Barry Wade, for his critical eye, and to Steve Forman, who set this project in motion at Norton. And my deep appreciation to Jerry Beaty and Paul Hunter for giving me this opportunity and for serving as my gracious mentors.

Jenny N. Sullivan

WRITING THEMES
ABOUT LITERATURE

A Guide to Accompany
The Norton Introduction to Literature
        Third Edition / Shorter Third Edition

Writing Themes about Literature

1

A General Guide and Handbook

A good thing ought to be shared. Sharing increases the pleasure of it. If you have ever dragged a friend to a movie that you decided he must see or if you have ever sent someone a copy of a good book you wanted her to read, then you know the pleasure of sharing literature. Most of us want to talk with others about what we have read; we want to hear other people's reactions and to offer our own opinions. It's almost as if the experience of reading is not complete until we have shared it.

Writing about literature is a way of sharing literature. When you write essays about works of literature that you have been studying, you are sharing your pleasures and insights with your audience. It's fun to show people what you know and to tell them what you think.

Writing about literature brings other pleasures too. Because the writing forces you to consider your views thoughtfully and to choose your words carefully, you will discover more in any work as you fine-tune your initial reactions and observations. A good piece of literature will give you something new each time you read and study it, and you will see more to enjoy in it than you did before. Writing about literature is hard work, but it is satisfying work that stems from the pleasure of sharing.

Writing a literary theme will be like writing any other essay in many specific ways, and all your literature papers will present similar challenges. How you begin a literary essay, how you incorporate quotations from the works, how you refer to the author, and how you develop evidence will not vary greatly from one assignment to another. This chapter will give you a general guide to the literary theme and to the parts that compose it.

Read through this chapter first, before you begin your paper; later you will want to return to this chapter for reference. You may find the need to refer to it time and again if you run into any snags in composing papers for your class.

GETTING READY TO WRITE

Marking the Text

As you read through the poem, short story, or play you will be writing about, mark your text, making notes and underlining passages. Use a pen or pencil or a highlighter, as you wish, but write all over your book. These notes will prove to be invaluable. Mark whatever your intellect or instinct tells you to. Consider the following ways of marking passages and the kinds of markings you might use.

1. Underline phrases that point to ideas you suspect are important to understanding the theme or following the plot.
2. Put question marks by words or phrases you do not fully understand. If something confuses you, write your question in the margin: "How come?" "Why is she doing this?" "How does he know this?" If there is a term you do not understand, look it up and write a definition in the margin. If you do not write down the definition, you will probably find yourself having to look up the same word again.
3. If you start to notice a pattern of words or images or ideas, underline the words or phrases that seem basic to it, or bracket the passage and make a note in the margins.

> I lingered before her stall, though I knew my stay was useless, to make my interest in her wares seem the more real. Then I turned away slowly and walked down the middle of the bazaar. I allowed the two pennies to fall against the sixpence in my pocket. I heard a voice call from one end of the gallery that the light was out. The upper part of the hall was now completely dark.
>
> Gazing up into the darkness I saw myself as a creature driven and derided by vanity, and my eyes burned with anguish and anger.

light and dark are mentioned in every scene

> Great oaks, more monumentally great oaks now
> Than ever when the living rose was new

mentions roses again

> HAMLET Ay, truly, for the power of beauty will sooner transform honesty from what it is to a bawd than the force of honesty can translate beauty into his likeness.

Hamlet talks about honesty and appearances to everyone

4. In a long or complex work, you may want to note the introduction of new characters by placing their names in the margin when they first appear.
5. As you see undertones in a character's speech, note your reactions to and conclusions about them: "Seems hostile." "Prideful." "Is he joking?"
6. If one work of literature reminds you of another work you have been studying, whether in its characters, its symbols, or its themes, make a note: "Sounds like Huck Finn." "Is this another death-wish poem?"

7. Mark points in the plot to help you refer to passages more easily: "This is background." "Flashback to the war." "Aha! She finally sees the light."

For what other reasons might you mark passages in your textbook? What you mark and how you mark it are entirely up to you since these notes are exclusively for *your* benefit.

Exercise

1. In a group, review the markings and notes that different members made while reading the same work of literature. Discuss among yourselves your various markings. Why did you mark passages the way you did? What patterns emerged? Which markings turned out not to be significant? How could you determine the difference?
2. Read the following excerpts, marking passages as you go along and making notes in the margins about them. Compare your work with the work of other class members.

THE ROCKING-HORSE WINNER

There was a woman who was beautiful, who started with all the advantages, yet she had no luck. She married for love, and the love turned to dust. She had bonny children, yet she felt they had been thrust upon her, and she could not love them. They looked at her coldly, as if they were finding fault with her. And hurriedly she felt she must cover up some fault in herself. Yet what it was that she must cover up she never knew. Nevertheless, when her children were present, she always felt the center of her heart go hard. This troubled her, and in her manner she was all the more gentle and anxious for her children, as if she loved them very much. Only she herself knew that at the center of her heart was a hard little place that could not feel love, no, not for anybody. Everybody else said of her: "She is such a good mother. She adores her children." Only she herself, and her children themselves, knew it was not so. They read it in each other's eyes.

There were a boy and two little girls. They lived in a pleasant house, with a garden, and they had discreet servants, and felt themselves superior to anyone in the neighborhood.

Although they lived in style, they felt always an anxiety in the house. There was never enough money. The mother had a small income, and the father had a small income, but not nearly enough for the social position which they had to keep up. The father went into town to some office. But though he had good prospects, these prospects never materialized. There was always the grinding sense of the shortage of money, though the style was always kept up.

At last the mother said: "I will see if *I* can't make something." But she did not know where to begin. She racked her brains, and tried this thing and the other, but could not find anything successful. The failure made deep lines come into her face. Her children were growing up, they would have to go to school. There must be more money, there must be more money. The father, who was always very handsome and expensive in his tastes, seemed as if he never *would* be able to do anything worth doing. And the mother, who had a great belief in herself, did not succeed any better, and her tastes were just as expensive.

NUNS FRET NOT

Nuns fret not at their convent's narrow room;
And hermits are contented with their cells;
And students with their pensive citadels;
Maids at the wheel, the weaver at his loom,
Sit blithe and happy; bees that soar for bloom,
High as the highest Peak of Furness-fells,
Will murmur by the hour in foxglove bells:
In truth the prison, unto which we doom
Ourselves, no prison is: and hence for me,
In sundry moods, 'twas pastime to be bound
Within the sonnet's scanty plot of ground;
Pleased if some souls (for such there needs must be)
Who have felt the weight of too much liberty,
Should find brief solace there, as I have found.

Posing a Thesis

As you read and mark your text, you are doing the groundwork for developing a thesis for your essay. The reactions and interpretations that you are putting into your marginal notes are the beginning of some statement you will make as the main point of the essay you write. What do your notes suggest about possible topics for an essay? What patterns are you seeing? What about the literature interests you? The kernel of the idea for your essay is somewhere in your notes.

For example, as you review your marginal notes on a certain short story, you might discover you have marked many passages for their religious overtones. You noted that the story is set in a Roman Catholic town, that the main character lives in a house where a priest has died, and that the girl with whom he is in love is described as having almost a halo around her as he sees her standing in the light of the doorway. These notes might lead you to scour the text for other examples and to conclude that the point of the story and of the action of the main character involves a pilgrimage of sorts. Clearly a study of religious imagery in the story would make a good paper topic with this thesis: Religious imagery in James Joyce's *Araby* helps to convey the spiritual intensity of a young boy's first love.

The thesis at this point is tentative. It may turn out to be a good one or a poor one; it may need adjusting. But it is a starting point. You won't know how good a topic it is until you try to gather evidence for it and thus test it.

Exercise

Review the marginal notes you made in the previous exercise. List two paper topics your notes suggest for each work of literature. Explain your answers.

The Rocking-Horse Winner
1.
2.
"Nuns Fret Not"
1.
2.

Gathering Evidence

No matter what kind of paper you are writing, you will need to make specific reference to the text of the poem, short story, or play you are writing about as a part of the evidence you introduce in support of your thesis. You may find it helpful to make note of especially apt quotations from the work of literature that you might want to incorporate into your essay. Following each quotation you make note of, you will want to have the page reference and your comment about the circumstances and significance of the quotation. Not only will your comments help you remember how you may want to use the material when the time comes, they are also the beginning of your argument in defense of your thesis. If you find it difficult to locate suitable passages, it may be that your thesis is faulty. Look at these passages and comments about *Young Goodman Brown*:

1. "... after this one night I'll cling to her skirts and follow [Faith] to heaven." (p. 118)

   Although Brown is talking about his wife Faith, the double meaning of her name suggests he is turning away from religious faith also, just for a while, he says.

2. "You are late, Goodman Brown."
   "Faith kept me back awhile." (p. 118)

   Double meaning again suggests his slipping away from religious faith.

3. "But, where is Faith?" (p. 124)

   Brown asks about his wife when he sees the townspeople at the Black Mass. Could he be asking also where is their faith? his faith?

If you have some quotations at hand and if you've already analyzed them *in writing*, the preparation of your paper will be that much easier. You may want to use note cards for gathering this evidence; then, when you prepare your outline, you can easily shuffle the ideas around by rearranging the notecards.

Making an Outline

Outlines for specific types of papers will be discussed separately in later chapters; for now, keep in mind that the value of making even a simple outline of your work is that the essay has a better chance of moving more easily and logically from section to section. You are more likely to develop all your paragraphs effectively from a central idea if you have worked out the organization ahead of time. A simple outline might include these basic elements:

INTRODUCTION
• Thesis statement indicating the purpose of the paper
• Statement of procedure indicating the paper's pattern of organization

BODY
• Topic sentence reiterating thesis and introducing first category of discussion
• ____   detail to develop the idea of the
  ____   topic sentence
  ____

• Next topic sentence . . .

CONCLUSION
• (Frankly, this is hard to plan ahead of time.)

COMPOSING THE DRAFT

Before you begin the actual writing of the first draft of your essay, you should have some sense of the writing process itself and an overview of the form and function of the parts of the essay.

Make yourself as comfortable as you can without going overboard (a soft bed or a sunny beach might be a touch too comfortable). Have your text, notecards, outline, pencils, paper, erasers, trashcan, rootbeer can, and anything else you need right at hand. Imagine that your ankles are chained to the chair and get a draft written all the way through with no interruptions. Getting revved-up—each and every time you have to do it—is the hard part; once you gather your momentum, the force of it helps to crystallize your ideas and get your assignment done. When you are on a roll, don't stop until you're finished. There is no better feeling than picking up a sheaf of scribbled papers and enjoying the relief of no longer having to carry all those heavy thoughts in your weary brain.

Before you throw yourself into the frenzy of composing, however, review this discussion of audience and the parts of the essay so that your second draft will be for polishing and not for starting all over again.

Tailoring Your Essay to a Specific Audience

Write for an audience that includes more people than just your teacher. Provide enough explanation so that someone who is not in your class and did not hear the assignment can appreciate the purpose of your essay. In other words, your writing should be self-contained; it should explain itself without making the reader feel the need to ask you for additional information to understand your point. You should write to an audience with education and maturity equal to your own.

The relationship between you and the audience is formal enough that you address them with the reserve you use for those who are not your close friends. But there is no need to be stuffy in your rhetoric; such a style would not make for very pleasant reading. On the other hand, slang or jargon would direct your paper only to some small group while alienating many others. A polite and informal style is best.

Consider the purpose of each assignment and how much your audience needs to be informed and about what. Are you acquainting them with the piece of literature or simply referring to a work with which the audience should be familiar? In most essays about literature, you will assume that your reader has read the work but has not appreciated the significance of the points you raise. Be sure not to expect too much of your audience. They will not have thought as long and hard about your subject as you have. What may be obvious to you by the writing of your final draft may nevertheless require explanation even to an intelligent, well read audience.

No one, except perhaps your teacher, is obliged to read what you write, but you should not take his or her interest for granted. You must draw an audience by making the reading of your essay a pleasant experience.

Exercise

Read through the following writing samples and choose the one with the most appropriate style for the audience reading a student essay in a literature class. What is wrong with the styles of the other two? How might they affect the audience?

1. Although Macomber is blessed with a fine countenance and need not worry after pecuniary matters, being wealthy enough to secure the commitment, through the bonds of holy matrimony, of a woman endowed with a more than comely face, he perceives himself to be altogether inadequate. Having shown himself to be ignobly frightened during the hunt, he suffered Margo's uxorial disdain and the manly Wilson's mute displeasure, nay, disgust. He stands in trepidation at the disapproval of others more than at the threat of lions and buffalo. He is a being in search of self-actualization.

2. Although Macomber is handsome and wealthy,
wealthy enough to "buy" a beautiful wife, he
feels inadequate. He was a coward during the
hunt and had to suffer Margo's insults and
Wilson's mute disgust. He fears the disapproval of others as much as the physical threat of
the lions and buffalo. He is a man who needs to
prove himself.

3. Although Macomber is good lookin' and has
enough bread to land a babe like Margo, he
feels like a jerk. When he acted like a chicken
during the hunt, his old lady and Mr. Macho let
him know what a creep they thought he was. He's
more shook by their putdowns than he is by the
thought of being wasted by some jungle creature
from the black lagoon. He needs to show 'em all
what a tough guy he really is.

Composing the Introduction of the Essay

Once you have a sense of audience, you are ready to plan
what goes into the three parts of the essay: the introduction,
the body, and the conclusion.

The length of the introduction of your essay will depend
upon the length and complexity of your paper. A three-page
essay might need only one paragraph of introduction. A
twenty-page essay might require six paragraphs to develop
its introduction. For convenience, the discussion here will
refer to introductions that are only one paragraph long.
What is important, however, is to think of the parts and
functions of your introduction, no matter how many paragraphs it takes to compose it.

As in any essay, the opening of a literary essay is used to
attract your readers, to create in them an immediate interest
in your subject. It promises that that interest will be re-
warded by the discussion that follows in the body of the
essay. If you learn to use the content and style of the open-

ing to your advantage, this part may be the most exciting to compose.

Content of the Opening. Remember that an opening should arouse readers by amusing them, challenging them, taking them by surprise—involving them immediately. What you say to begin your essay should, of course, complement the purpose of your essay. The following questions will guide you in selecting material for an effective opening.

1. Is there a particular passage or scene in the literary work that seems to sum up the main idea or highlight it dramatically?
2. Is there a nagging question that the work leaves in the mind of the conscientious reader?
3. Is there a particularly striking image or turn of phrase in the work that would make a good opener?
4. Is there a typical first response that many readers might have had to the work that calls for comment? For example, is the story sad or gory or frightening? Is it elusive and difficult to follow?
5. Does the main idea of the literary work speak to a current political, social, or moral issue?

Exercise

As a class, discuss the answers to these questions as they apply to the following works of literature. Then try writing a crisp and engaging opening sentence for several different possible papers on one of these works:

1. *The Dumb Waiter*
2. *Boys and Girls*
3. "To an Athlete Dying Young"

Style of the Opening. Just as the content should be provocative in order to entice your reader, so too should your style engage your audience. You can make your sentence structures attractive with special attention to syntax—the ordering of words—and a careful use of punctuation to high-light the effect of the syntax. As you lead your reader into the substance of your essay, why not make the journey as pleasant and inviting as possible? Unusually short sentences, unusually long sentences, or a striking combination of both can attract your reader's attention, as can an arrangement of words out of the ordinary subject-verb-object pattern or sentences with parallel structure.

```
The time is out of joint. O curséd spite        striking
That ever I was born to set it right!           passage
                                                quoted
```

```
    Thus agonizes the young prince in William   long
Shakespeare's Hamlet as he wrestles with his    sentence
                                                followed
responsibility to avenge his father's murder.   by two
No longer can he be a carefree youth. No ) parallel  short
longer is his life purely his own.        sentence  sentences
                                          openings
```

Syntax that incorporates the use of dramatic marks of punctuation, such as the colon or the dash, can enhance the opening if used sparingly to create a special effect. Observe how the syntax of the example below builds dramatically to the colon, which sets off the powerful one-word, appositive ending.

```
    Edgar Allan Poe's The Cask of Amontillado
deals with one of the darkest of human
impulses: revenge.
```

Your opening is also the place to begin establishing key words and phrases that will recall your main points throughout the essay.

Exercise

1. Read and comment on the content and style of this opening. Is it effective or not? Explain.

```
    Dulce et decorum est pro patria mori.
    It is sweet and proper to die for one's
country.
```

This old saying is a lie, according to Wilfred Owen in his poem, "Dulce et Decorum Est." The poem suggests that, whatever else it might be, dying for one's country in war is certainly ugly and horrible to watch. The poem uses powerful descriptive words and images to depict this horror. The impact of the images and the connotations of the words of the speaker reinforce the theme as they show an awful gas attack on a group of war-weary soldiers on the march.

2. Rewrite this opening to improve its style.

Irony in "Ozymandias"
The central theme in Percy Bysshe Shelley's poem "Ozymandias" is in itself an irony. Ozymandias was a powerful Egyptian king who was so certain that his power would last that he had colossal statues with boastful inscriptions sculpted. However powerful Ozymandias was in his day, time has eroded his reputation and his statues. Now the proud inscriptions serve only to make a mockery of the king who was so certain that his grandeur would survive him. As the speaker in the poem observes, "Nothing beside remains." Shelley further develops this central ironic theme by describing the ironic setting, situations, and thoughts that surround this "King of Kings," Ozymandias.

Developing a Thesis Statement in the Introduction

Your thesis is the *central idea of your essay.* It is not the central idea of the work of literature. What are *you* trying to accomplish in *your* essay? What will *you* discuss? What is *your* slant, *your* angle, *your* point? Put this information in your thesis. The thesis is the business end of your introduction. Once you have gained your audience's interest with your opening, you should clearly and fully explain the paper's purpose without mechanically saying, "I will next prove that . . . "

The thesis should focus the writing for your readers and guide their understanding of your discussion. But just as often, a good thesis focuses your writing, helping you to keep to the point and to write with direction and purpose.

Read the opening paragraph cited in the last exercise again, this time with an eye to thesis.

<u>Dulce et decorum est pro patria mori</u>.
It is sweet and dignified to die for one's country.
This old saying is a lie, according to Wilfred Owen in his poem, "Dulce et Decorum Est." The poem suggests that, whatever else it might be, dying for one's country in war is certainly ugly and horrible to watch. The poem uses powerful descriptive words and images to depict this horror. The impact of the images and the connotations of the words of the speaker reinforce the theme as they show an awful gas attack on a group of war-weary soldiers on the march.

} thesis

} statement of procedure

"The poem uses powerful words and images to depict this horror": The thesis sentence tells a reader that the essay will analyze specific "words" and "images" that the student will show to be "powerful" in depicting the "horror" of battle. If the essay does not then do what it says it will, it will not be a success, no matter how well it develops other worthwhile topics. A good thesis gives both you and your audience a sense of focus, purpose, and direction. It establishes for both of you key words or ideas that will appear throughout. It puts both of you in a frame of mind to deal with specific detail.

Reread the sentence that follows the thesis.

The impact of the images and the connotations of the words of the speaker reinforce the theme as they show an awful gas attack on a group of war-weary soldiers on the march.

It is an amplification of the thesis and what we might call a statement of procedure. It suggests the organization of the essay and of the paragraphs. It is more specific than the thesis, telling the reader that the essay will discuss the effect or "impact" of the images and the overtones or "connotations" of the words. It also reminds the reader that the purpose of this essay is to relate these ideas to the poem's theme of how horrible war is, a theme that the poet demonstrates through the example of a gas attack. The statement of procedure helps the writer to decide how to finally organize supporting detail. It is a transition to the first paragraph of the body.

Exercise

Read these thesis statements and explain in your own words what they tell you about the purpose of the essays from which they come.

1. Richard Connell's The Most Dangerous Game is a compelling story about the ordeals one man must endure as the "prey" in a hunt undertaken by a lunatic.
2. The setting in Nathaniel Hawthorne's Young Goodman Brown helps the reader appreciate how evil the journey this one young man takes really is.
3. The Glass Menagerie is the story of a fragile family.

Composing the Body of the Essay

The body of the essay is the most important part because that is where you provide explanation and detail to convince the reader of your point. The body contains the textual evidence and explains to your reader *how* your thesis applies to the work.

Discussing Evidence

Citing evidence and quoting passages is only part of what you will do in the paragraphs of the body of a literary essay. What will give the evidence meaning in your paper will be your explanatory, analytical, and synthesizing commentary. It is not enough to say that your evidence or quotation *is* an example of a particular point. You must explain *how* it is an example.

In this paragraph about Amanda Wingfield of Tennessee Williams's *The Glass Menagerie,* the student does not assume his audience will be able to analyze his example and see how it relates to his point. He analyzes it for us.

```
    Amanda expresses herself in a manner
reminiscent of the gentility of the lost past
for which she longs. She tells of the after-
noon she had seventeen "gentlemen callers."
These "planters and sons of planters" were
not mere "boyfriends" or "dates." They were
"gentlemen," back in an age of chivalry, who
came calling on refined young ladies in their
courtly fashion.
```

The topic sentence from the example above makes the general point that Amanda's manner of expression recalls a time of gentility for which she longs. Through discussion the student must explain *how* the examples reflect this manner. The student points out that the phrase "gentlemen callers" is not like "boyfriends" or "dates." It is more genteel, an old-fashioned expression from a lost past, which, the student explains, was a time of chivalry and courtliness. The suggestion is that there was a touch of refinement back then that is lost in the modern dating game.

It is important not to presume that what has become obvious to you through several readings of the work is obvious to your reader. Like a lawyer you must connect the evidence to your case, to your thesis. You must explain to your jury, the audience, the significance of your evidence. You don't hand them a set of fingerprints, a photograph of the rifling marks on a bullet, or the raw data from psychological tests without putting an expert witness on the stand to explain to them *how* this evidence is to be viewed. In your essay, you are not only the lawyer; you are also the expert witness.

Exercise

Drawing evidence from these quotations, practice writing sentences of commentary that link the evidence to the thesis posed in each example.

1. Explain how this passage demonstrates the excitement of being at a dance as Leila and her cousin in Katherine Mansfield's *Her First Ball* go to the ladies' room to primp before going out on the floor.

   Two benches on either side were stacked high with wraps. Two old women in white aprons ran up and down tossing fresh armfuls. And everybody was pressing forward trying to get at the little dressing table and mirror at the far end.

2. Develop several sentences explaining how Theodore Roethke, in "My Papa's Waltz," suggests that Papa was solid, working-class stock by saying that his hand was "battered on one knuckle" and his "palm crusted hard by dirt."

3. Explain how, in Adrienne Rich's "Aunt Jennifer's Tigers," the line in which the speaker tells us that when she dies "her terrified hands will lie / Still ringed with ordeals she was mastered by" reinforces the notion that Aunt Jennifer is not strong and bold like the figures in her needlework.

Organizing the Paragraphs of the Body

A paragraph in the body of a literary essay needs

- a topic sentence
- sentences with concrete detail

- unity
- transitions
- a pattern of logical order.

The topic sentence, usually the first sentence in your paragraph, should directly reflect the idea of your thesis and should repeat key ideas and words from the thesis. Remember the sample thesis statement discussed earlier in this chapter:

```
The poem uses powerful words and images to
depict this horror.
```

Here is the topic sentence for the first body paragraph:

```
    In the first section of the poem, even
before the frightful gas attack begins, Owen
uses his forceful language to show us a weary
band of soldiers.
```

This topic sentence

- reflects the thesis by paralleling words like "frightful" with "horror," "forceful language" with "powerful words," and "shows us" with "depicts"

and

- narrows the focus from the idea of the whole "poem" in the thesis to just "the first section" in this paragraph.

Important: The lead sentence of your paragraph should not simply give a detail of the plot or describe the first image in a poem. If you begin this way, you are likely to drift into a simple retelling of the work and drift away from your original purpose.

Now let's review the entire paragraph for organization and form.

In the first section of the poem, even before the frightful gas attack begins, Owens uses his forceful language to show us a weary band of soldiers. By concentrating on their physical appearance, he lets us see war's devastating effect on the men. They are not gloriously gleaming soldiers proudly strutting, but are "bent double, like old beggars" and are "coughing like hags." They "trudge" through the elements with difficulty, not at all boldly marching to battle.

Concrete detail.   Notice the numerous quotations and how they are woven in. Concrete detail in a paragraph of the body of a literary essay consists of such quotations and other specific references to particular characters, situations, relationships, and actions—*details*—of the work of literature.

Exercise

Read through this paragraph from the body of a literary essay and underline examples of concrete detail.

Ozymandias's diminished power is reemphasized in the irony of the actual situations surrounding the ruins that the speaker describes. There are huge fragments of what once stood as a colossal statue, tall and imposing and able to make its impression seemingly throughout time. The fierce glare of the statue's face, "the sneer of cold command," must have evoked fear in all who beheld it. What better way to assure the faithfulness of his subjects than for Ozymandias to have these features of strength recorded for posterity in stone. Now, however, the giant figure has been reduced to "trunkless legs of stone," disjointed from the head that lies half-buried in the sand. The commanding expression of the face no longer inspires fear but seems

almost humorous. In fact, it seems to
heighten the irony that Ozymandias is no
longer a demanding reality, but is instead
a decaying one.

Unity.   Observe how unity—singleness of purpose—is
achieved in the synthesizing explanatory notes of the student writing about Wilfred Owen's poem.

They "trudge" through the elements <u>with</u>
<u>difficulty</u>, <u>not</u> <u>at</u> <u>all</u> <u>boldly</u> <u>marching</u> <u>to</u>
<u>battle</u>.

The student is explaining, consistent with the idea of his
topic sentence, that the "forceful language" shows us a
"weary band of soldiers." The unifying factor in a paragraph is established by the key terms used in the topic sentence that identify the idea or point of the paragraph.
Whenever that idea appears in the sentences that follow, as
it always should, the unity of the paragraph is reinforced.
Notice that the student does not stray from the discussion of
"forceful language" used to describe a "weary band of soldiers." Had the student strayed, the paragraph would no
longer have been unified.

Exercise

Read again the paragraph on "Ozymandias" used in the
previous exercise. Underline key terms in the topic sentence. Then explain how the idea of each sentence that follows relates to those key terms and thus to the point of the
whole paragraph. Is the paragraph unified?

(1) Ozymandias's diminished power is
reemphasized in the irony of the actual
situations surrounding the ruins that the
speaker describes. (2) There are huge
fragments of what once stood as a colossal
statue, tall and imposing and able to make
its impression seemingly throughout time.

```
(3) The fierce glare of the statue's
face, "the sneer of cold command," must
have evoked fear in all who beheld it.
(4) What better way to assure the faith-
fulness of his subjects than for Ozymandias
to have these features of strength recorded
for posterity in stone. (5) Now, however,
the giant figure has been reduced to "trunk-
less legs of stone," disjointed from the
head that lies half-buried in the sand.
(6) The commanding expression of the face
no longer inspires fear but seems almost
humorous. (7) In fact, it seems to heighten
the irony that Ozymandias is no longer a
demanding reality, but is instead a decaying
one.
```

Transition or Linkage. Notice the use of "they,"
"their," and "them" to refer to the soldiers in the sample
paragraph on "Dulce et Decorum Est" that we have been
discussing. Notice also the many words akin to weariness.
Any words or phrases used to connect ideas from one sentence to another are transitions that link the sentences not
only in thought but in expression also. The phrasing of your
sentences should reinforce the unity of your thought by
linking ideas through transition.

Exercise

Read the following paragraph and underline key words
in the topic sentence and the sentence that follows it. Then
circle and draw arrows between words and phrases in the
subsequent sentences that link them in thought and expression to the topic sentence and to other sentences in the
paragraph.

```
Another feature of the play, character
development, is also superior. Tennessee
Williams takes Amanda, for example, and
makes her come alive with her dialogue, her
frustrations and motivations, and the way
```

she treats her children. Her language is
often that of the Southern Belle. She
reflects a refinement her life no longer has.
She no longer has "seventeen gentlemen callers"
or even one husband! Her daughter is not a
belle, and her son is a reminder of his father.
We see all these complex parts of her psychology in everything she says. We see it
when she advises Laura that "all pretty
girls are a trap, and men expect them to
be." We hear it again when she flirts with
Jim.

> Well, well, well, so this is Mr.
> O'Connor. Introductions entirely un-
> necessary. I've heard so much about you
> from my boy. I finally said to him,
> Tom--good gracious!--why don't you
> bring this paragon to supper.

And we are struck by her desperate tone
when she lashes out at Tom.

> That's right, now that you've had us
> make such fools of ourselves. The effort,
> the preparations, all the expense! The
> new floor lamp, the rug, the clothes for
> Laura! All for what? To entertain some
> other girl's fiancé! Go to the movies, go!

Amanda is a tortured woman whose wants
are excellently developed by a powerful
playwright.

Pattern of Logical Order.   Observe in our sample introductory paragraph for the essay on "Dulce et Decorum
Est" (p. 15) that the student writer analyzes the "forceful
language" of the poet in paragraphs that comment on particular words or phrases as each appears in sequence in the
poem.

You should always have a rationale for arranging sentences in a paragraph as you do. A simple sequence imitat-
ing the organization of what you are writing about is one

such pattern. Other patterns of logical order include, for instance, spatial arrangement, chronological order, moving from cause to effect, and, most importantly, moving from the least significant to the most significant idea.

Exercise

Read the sample paragraphs below and explain the writer's apparent reason for arranging the sentences as they are arranged. You may discover more than one pattern of logical order operating in each paragraph.

1. All of the themes in this play, which can generally be put under the heading of "facing reality," are important ones that most people can identify with. We all suffer one or more of the problems of the Wingfield family and try to escape them as they do. Most of us have some form of Laura's insecurities, especially as teenagers when it is so hard to accept imperfections in ourselves. The older we get, the more we find ourselves burdened with responsibilities like Tom's, which often seem to smother us as he felt smothered. "Man is by instinct a lover, a hunter, a fighter, and none of those instincts are given much play at a warehouse." When things get too bad, it is easy to drift into Amanda's kind of golden memories embroidered to be more beautiful than the past really was. We see her escape into bygone times when she exclaims to Laura, "This is the dress in which I led the Cotillion. Won the cakewalk twice at Sunset Hill, wore one Spring to the Governor's Ball in Jackson!" The themes in this play are about everyday experiences that mean a great deal to people. It is about how people live their lives and see themselves.

2. Upon their arrival at Montresor's house, there are hints that evil lurks,

that Montresor's revenge has been carefully
planned. He has made sure the house is
empty, and he is overly generous in plying
Fortunato with wine, "Medoc against the
damp." We watch as Montresor leads the
drunken Fortunato further and deeper into
the catacombs, damp, stifling chambers of
death with a "foulness of air." This for-
boding journey continues until Montresor
leads Fortunato into a dark crypt by a
pile of bones where the Amontillado is
supposedly stored. But Fortunato discovers
that there is none there.

Composing the Conclusion of the Essay

Any closing paragraph should not simply restate your
thesis word for word but should reassert that idea and
sound a note of finality. It should imitate what you hear in
the voice of the speaker when you know it's time to get your
car keys out because you will be going home soon: "And so,
my friends, I leave you with this thought. Vote for me!"

The closing, like the opening, is a dramatic point in your
essay. What you say here and how you say it should do justice to the whole essay. Your paper deserves a nice finish-
ing touch.

Content of the Closing.   The material in your essay
should suggest your conclusion. Ask yourself the following
questions in deciding how to close your essay.

1. Is your essay long and complex enough to warrant a summary?
2. Has the essay built up to a specific generalization or
   philosophical position you should assert in closing?
3. Is there a passage from the text of the literature that really
   ought to be the last word?
4. Does your discussion lead to a final question that you
   wish to pose to your reader?

5. Or does your final example tie matters up? Would it be anticlimactic to say more, to have a separate concluding paragraph?

Do not end your essay by just stopping dead in your tracks or by introducing ideas you do not intend to develop. The lingering last impression is important.

Style of the Closing.   Just as considerations of unusual punctuation and unusual sentence structure help you stimulate the reader in your opening, they can help your conclusion too. Dramatic, emphatic sentences—usually short ones—and punctuation that breaks longer sentences into short, emphatic units work well in a closing. Read the following paragraph aloud and listen. These are the final few sentences from an interpretive summary paper (one in which the writer explains plot in terms of the story's theme—revenge).

short sentence followed by a longer one then by another short one for a closing punch

> And there is "impunity" in Montresor's revenge. He tells us that for a "half century no mortal has disturbed" that pile of bones and discovered his evil deed. He has committed the perfect crime!

dramatic punctuation in a short, assertive statement summing up the story

REVISING AND POLISHING THE DRAFT

Once you have in hand that wonderful sheaf of scribbled papers that constitute a first draft, relax and let go for a while. Bask in the glory of having produced this great work, and don't even think about revising or polishing it for at least one day. You and your essay deserve a rest; you will both be better off in the long run if you part company for a while.

When your day of vacation is over, take that rough-cut diamond in hand again and prepare to polish it into a thing of beauty that will be a joy forever. Read over your draft with an eye to improving the essay's sense, organization, style, and correctness.

Read your draft with your newly acquired sense of distance to see if it all still makes sense. You may decide that you need to delete some ideas, add others, expand still others, and rearrange some. Ideas may need beefing up with details and examples. Some may have become tedious through overdevelopment. Make what adjustments you need so that your paper reads well.

Look at your organizing statements and read for basic essay coherence. Do the thoughts hang together and proceed clearly and logically through the paragraphs? Does your thesis remain central throughout the essay?

Read for style and correctness. Smooth out any awkwardnesses; correct the improper structures; and check your punctuation and spelling.

Make sure also that your paper adheres to the following conventions of the literary essay dealing with tense, reference to the author and work, incorporation of quotations, form of the title, and manuscript form.

Using Proper Tense

As you discuss the events occurring in the work of literature, use the present tense.

```
As the story opens, Goodman Brown  is
bidding his wife Faith goodbye.
```

When you refer to events that happened before the beginning of the story, things the characters or narrator refer to as a part of the past, use the appropriate past tense.

```
Brown  had made  an appointment to meet with
the Devil in the forest and  is  intent on
keeping it.
```

Making Reference to the Author
and the Literary Work

• Somewhere in your introduction, the title and author of the work under study should be named. While your audience may in fact be only your teacher, who knows what works you are writing about, you should never take it for granted that even that reader is certain about your subject. Your teacher may be reading essays on several different works in a short period of time.

• The first time you mention the author, give the full name as it appears in your text: Emily Dickinson, F. Scott Fitzgerald, A. E. Housman, Lady Catherine Dyer. After this, use the author's last name only, without title, whenever you make references: Dickinson, Fitzgerald, Housman. Note, however, that some names require special treatment. For instance, George Gordon, Lord Byron, is referred to as Byron; Lady Catherine Dyer is referred to as Lady Catherine; and Gabriel García Márquez is called García Márquez. Whenever you are uncertain about the proper way to refer to an author, check with your instructor or librarian to learn what is customary.

• Remember that in your reference to the work of literature you will place quotation marks around the full, complete, and accurate titles of poems and will underline titles of short stories and plays. (Conventions differ; your teacher may give you another set of instructions on this point.)

• The subtitle of a work of literature is indicated by placing a colon between it and the main title.

"The River Merchant's Wife: A Letter"

Exercise

Which of these titles call for quotation marks in your essay references to them? Which call for underlining?

1. A Hunger Artist
2. Do Not Go Gentle into That Good Night
3. Barbie Doll

4. Hamlet
5. Araby

If the title has an end mark of punctuation that will not fit coherently in your sentence structure, the punctuation mark may be omitted.

```
In Elizabeth Barrett Browning's "How Do
I Love Thee," we hear the speaker proclaim . . .
```

Incorporating Quotations

The best proof that a work of literature does what you say it does is textual evidence: words and sentences you can cite from the poem, story, or play you are discussing. If you say that a character in a story is evil, can you quote a passage in which he clearly says or does something evil or a passage in which a reliable character or narrator talks of his evil? The best support you have as you discuss a literary work is the text of the work itself.

As you incorporate textual evidence into your discussion through the use of quotations, there are some rules you should keep in mind.

1. Do not overuse quotations. The style of your writing will be better if you incorporate quoted phrases into your own sentence structure rather than writing a sentence and then quoting a sentence or poetic line.

```
Richard Cory was very polite. "He was a           ineffective
gentleman from sole to crown." Also he
was good-looking, even regal-looking--
"clean favored, and imperially slim."

Richard Cory was polite, "a gentleman from        effective
sole to crown." Like a handsome king he was
"clean favored, and imperially slim."
```

2. Avoid having two quotations in a row. Your own commentary should bridge the two.

ineffective

```
Richard Cory had everything going for him.
"He was a gentleman from sole to crown."
"And he was rich--yes, richer than a king."
```

effective

```
Richard Cory had everything going for him.
Not only was he a "gentleman from sole to
crown"; he was also "richer than a king."
```

3. Work the quotation comfortably into your sentence structure.

ineffective

```
"Darkened by the gloomiest of trees" shows
just how frightening the forest looked.
```

effective

```
The forest, "darkened by the gloomiest of
trees," was a frightening place.
```

4. Longer quotations (more than two lines of verse or four lines of prose) should be set off from your paragraph in display form: single-spaced and centered without quotation marks.

```
Dickinson describes the numbness that comes
with the shock of the loss of a loved one:

    The Nerves sit ceremonious, like Tombs--
    The stiff Heart questions was it He,
        that bore,
    And Yesterday, or Centuries before?
```

5. Separate lines of poetry running within your sentences with a slash (/), and preserve the capitalization of words at the beginning of the line.

```
The speaker notes that the bruised heart
of the mourner wonders "was it He, that
bore, / And Yesterday, or Centuries before?"
```

6. You may alter the punctuation and capitalization of a quotation to conform to the needs of your sentence structure, as long as you do not alter the meaning of the lines.

```
He was a gentleman from sole to crown,
Clean favored, and imperially slim.
```
original lines of poetry

```
Richard Cory, "clean favored, and imperially
slim," was from head to toe a gentleman.
```
alterations of punctuation and capitalization required by the student's sentence structure

7. If, for clarity or sentence structure, you must alter a quotation, place the alteration in brackets.

```
With Heaven above and Faith below, I will
yet stand firm against the devil.
```
original lines
```
1. Goodman Brown claims that "with Heaven
   above and Faith below, [he] will yet stand
   firm against the devil."
2. Goodman Brown hoped that "with Heaven
   above and Faith below, [he would] yet
   stand firm against the devil."
```
alterations for clarity and consistency in sentence structure

8. If you omit material in order to be succinct, mark the omission by three periods (called an ellipsis) with a space between each (. . .). *Note:* There is no need to use these routinely at the beginning and end of your quotations. It is understood that you are lifting passages from a longer work.

```
Montresor tells us that when it came to
"painting and gemmary, Fortunato . . . was
a quack."
```

9. Be sure to name the source of the quotation correctly.
   • In nonnarrative poetry (poetry in which characters do not appear in a plot), it is correct to say "The speaker says . . ." not "The poet says . . ."

• In a story with a narrator, it is correct to say "The narrator says . . . " when quoting passages of narration, not "The author says . . . "

• Identify characters as you quote them.

```
In Thomas Hardy's "Channel Firing," God
answers the people in their graves with
"Ha, ha. It will be warmer when / I blow
the trumpet."
```

• When quoting dialogue between characters in a play, set if off and begin a new line as you quote each character. Place the character's name in front of his line.

```
Later in the play Hamlet confronts his
mother:

  HAMLET: Now, mother, what's the
          matter?
  QUEEN:  Hamlet, thou hast thy father
          much offended.
```

Developing a Title

Your title gives your reader his very first impression of your essay. Take time to find an appropriate and imaginative one.

• Create a title for your essay that indicates your purpose. The title can be very businesslike

Irony in "Ozymandias"

or a bit more provocative

The Despair of "Ozymandias": A Study in Irony

• Simply using the title of the work isn't very helpful. The title of the work conveys nothing about your essay's particular subject, slant, or theme, as the essay's title should.

• Capitalize the major words of your title. *Do not* put your essay's title in quotation marks and *do not* underline it.

> Irony in "Ozymandias"
> not "Irony in 'Ozymandias' "
> not <u>Irony in "Ozymandias"</u>

Quotation marks appear around "Ozymandias" because that is the title of the poem.

• The title of a short story or play is underlined when you refer to it in the title or the body of your essay.

• No period appears at the end of your title. As a general rule, titles are not complete sentences.

• Sometimes, but rarely, a title might be a question with a question mark at the end.

> Why Is It So Important to Be Earnest?

Using Proper Manuscript Form

Your manuscript, your final draft, should be presented with care—a neat-looking paper is more pleasing to read than a sloppy one. Moreover, rightly or wrongly, a sloppy paper suggests that the writer cares little about his work.

While your instructor may make specific manuscript requirements, here are a few standard guidelines.

1. Use regular-weight, white 8½ by 11 inch typing paper or, if you are handwriting your assignment, wide-line loose-leaf paper.
2. Use only one side of the paper.
3. Use blue, black, or blue-black ink for handwritten papers. Use a clean black ribbon for typed work. Double-space your typing.
4. Center your title.
5. Skip a line between your title and the first paragraph of your essay.
6. Make all margins at least one inch; the left-hand margin may be 1½ inches.
7. Indent the first line of each paragraph one inch or use block paragraphs, skipping an extra line between them.

8. Number all pages *except* the first. Place page numbers in the upper right-hand corner with no parentheses, hyphens, or periods around or behind them.
9. Break words at the end of a syllable if you must hyphenate at the end of a line. *Do not* hyphenate unless you have at least three letters to carry down.
10. Begin no line with a mark of punctuation; end no line with an opening quotation mark, bracket, or parenthesis.
11. Paper clip the pages in the upper left-hand corner.
12. Carat (∧) in omissions. Delete by marking through with a single line. Recopy any page that requires more than three corrections. But remember, if you must choose, it is better to be correct than neat.
13. Ask your instructor what identifying information in addition to your name you should provide and where it should appear.

A Final Reminder.   The material in this chapter applies to all the types of essays the later chapters discuss. Use this chapter as a handbook. If one part of an essay is giving you a particular problem, review the discussion and exercises contained here.

Summarizing and Explicating Literature

2

You may never be asked to write an interpretive summary, at least as a separate essay assignment. But summarizing is almost always a part of any major paper about literature and is very often used as a study exercise. You have certainly encountered literary summaries in your everyday reading and have depended on them more than you may realize. Movie, theatre, and book reviews you read in newspapers or magazines often begin with a summary of the plot of the story. Daily television listings offer ten- or fifteen-word summaries of the shows on the air. You may have even found yourself buying a twenty-page condensed version of *Moby Dick* or *War and Peace* to have a quick summary of that long novel you are reading.

There are two important ideas to draw from these examples. First, readers depend on summaries to be accurate. Whether you are deciding if you want to spend money on a particular movie, spend time watching a certain TV show, or spend energy reading a book, you expect the writer of the summary to give you correct information. Second, the length of a summary can vary greatly according to the needs of the audience. One line may be sufficient to summarize a televised play in the TV listings; a review of that show by a television critic for the same newspaper may begin with a three-paragraph summary; a summary of the same play for an English class assignment may take five pages. The length always depends on the purpose and the audience. The writer of a summary needs to keep a clear sense of purpose and of proportion. This chapter will deal with essay-length summaries, but the principles apply to most any summary.

Exercise

Other than the examples given above, where else have you seen summaries? Look, for example, at textbooks for other courses. Do they have chapter summaries? How long are they? What purpose(s) do they serve? List and describe the form and purpose of three summaries you have found in your daily reading.

WHAT THEME IS—AND IS NOT

Why would your teacher ask you to summarize a poem, short story, or play? The first response to come to your mind might be, "To make sure I read the material." While in fact that might be one of the reasons you are asked to write a summary, it is not the most important one. As a student of literature, you should practice summarizing a work because summarizing forces you to read closely and attentively in order to find the *unifying theme* of the literature, the theme that makes all its parts relate to one another. Anyone who writes a good summary of a work understands that work, in its totality, better than he or she did before.

The theme of a work of literature is like the central idea or thesis of an essay. And just as all the paragraphs of an essay should clearly and directly relate to the central idea, so too should all the actions and images of a poem or story or play relate to its theme. Learning to recognize this relationship is important for your growth as a student of literature. Demonstrating your understanding of this relationship is what writing interpretive summaries is all about. As you begin to read a work, you need to think about what you are reading to discover the central idea, the major theme. What is it about life, human nature, the condition of humankind that this work is discussing? *Do not look for a lesson.* You are likely not to find one. Many authors are not trying to teach us anything in the sense that they expect to alter our conduct. They simply want to show us something, help us see or feel something more clearly than we did before. Emily Dickinson's "After Great Pain" vividly describes the emotional stages people go through after the loss of someone dear. She teaches no lessons, however, and gives us no remedies. Her purpose is to reveal emotions. Even readers who have never lost a loved one can better understand what that experience is like. Those readers who have lost someone often respond very strongly and deeply to how beautifully and precisely she has articulated something they themselves have felt; or they might respond to an emotional state unlike their own, but a state with which they can sympathize because Dickinson gives something against which to measure their own grief. Dickinson's readers are moved, touched in some way, but they are not given a lesson or simple moral platitude.

Whether on TV or in a magazine or book, you may encounter a work that does offer such a moral: "There's good and evil in everyone"; "Happiness and success can come to the undeserving as well as to the worthy"; and so forth. If that's all that the work offers, however, you probably won't remember it for very long or ever reread it. Rather than read a poem or story or play to glean such unexciting news, you might just as well read a fortune cookie.

Even Aesop's fables, which are well known for their morals, stick in our minds as much for their characters and situations as for their theme. The theme of "The Tortoise and the Hare" may be "slow but steady wins the race," but don't the personalities of the two animals and maneuvers of the race give even so brief a fable more meaning than just the simple moral?

Most of the works you read in your literature class will be rich and complex; and while after much careful reading and thought you will be able to point to an underlying theme, you will discover that this theme does not reduce a work to a simple platitude but becomes a key to further appreciating the work's richness.

Exercise

1. Review the poetry section of the table of contents of your textbook. What themes are used to group some of the poems? What subject matters serve as headings? Express the theme of several of the poems more fully.
2. Select a poem from one of these groups and explain, in a paragraph, why the poem has been placed under that particular heading. Be specific in your answer, making direct reference to details of the poem.
3. Select two poems listed under the same heading. Read and explain how each treats their common theme differently.

FINDING THE THEME OF A WORK OF LITERATURE

To a large extent, finding the theme of a work of literature is what your whole English course is about. Discovering theme is no simple process, but it is a most rewarding one.

If this discussion suggests you ought to find the process simple, but you do not, take heart; discovering theme is hard work for everyone.

Some works of literature have a single theme that they may hand us in a neat phrase, such as Herrick's "Delight in Disorder." It would not be incorrect to say that this poem is about how delightful disorder in a woman's appearance can be. Other works do not make matters quite so easy for us. Shakespeare's *Hamlet*, for instance, has many themes that we find as they are slowly spun out in a complicated story line. The play deals with revenge, loyalty, reluctance, appearances, love, and many other weighty subjects and ideas. It would be more difficult to write a good summary of *Hamlet* than of a shorter and simpler work such as "Delight in Disorder." While some works may offer simple moral platitudes, it would be unwise for you to assume that all works of literature will. Most of the literature you will be assigned in your English class is richer and more complex than literature that offers easy morals.

Exercise

Each of the following works of literature has more than one theme. List as many themes for each as is appropriate and explain briefly how you arrived at your answers.

1. *The Secret Sharer*
2. *Her First Ball*
3. "Stopping by Woods on a Snowy Evening"
4. *Hedda Gabler*
5. *Oedipus Tyrannus*
6. "The Death of the Ball Turret Gunner"
7. "Pied Beauty"
8. "London"

As you set about to discover the theme of a work of literature, you need to establish a hypothesis as soon as you can. Begin at the very beginning: the title. The reader who pauses for a moment to consider Herrick's title "Delight in Disorder" begins with a hypothesis about the poem's theme that is proved right. The title always tells you *some-thing*, even if it proves to be misleading. *The Most Danger-ous Game* may make you think of rugby or skydiving before you begin the story. After you start reading, however, you realize that *game* is meant another way. But by the end of the story, it's clear that the title is a pun, that *both* meanings are intended, and that the story's theme is tied up with the title's implications.

What do you make of the first line or sentence or speech of the work? The first line of *Hamlet* is "Who's there?" Shakespeare could have begun in any fashion; why begin this way? What guesses can you make about the play from this single question—that it is a play of uncertainty? a play about identity? Maxine Kumin's "Woodchucks" begins, "Gassing the woodchucks didn't turn out right." *Gassing* is a rather unusual word here, isn't it? The word will not be used again until the last line of the poem (as *gassed*), and it's clear that this word is important to the theme of the poem. If you have taken a moment to consider the first word of this poem, even a first reading should help you pick out words and images important to Kumin's theme.

But if you don't already know what the theme is, how can you form your hypothesis? As soon as you discover an idea that you think may be the theme, focus on it. Read with that idea in mind, testing your hypothesis. If it is confirmed by the rest of the story, your reading will be a collecting of evidence. If the story moves in another direction and your hypothesis proves to be wrong, reading with this kind of concentration will nevertheless make the true theme easier to discover.

Read the first paragraph of Poe's "The Cask of Amontillado."

> The thousand injuries of Fortunato I had borne as I best could, but when he ventured upon insult I vowed revenge. You, who so well know the nature of my soul, will not suppose, however, that I gave utterance to a threat. *At length* I would be avenged; this was a point definitely settled—but the very definitiveness with which it was resolved precluded the idea of risk. I must not only punish but punish with impunity. A wrong is unredressed when retribution overtakes its redresser. It is equally unredressed when the avenger fails to make himself felt as such to him who has done the wrong.

What seems to be the narrator's preoccupation? Are there any words that are repeated? Ideas repeated? Could these suggest a hypothesis about the theme?

If you were reading carefully and with concentration, you should have noticed "revenge," "avenge," "punish with impunity," and "retribution." This story is, in fact, a story of "revenge" and "retribution," of a man who avenges himself by punishing "with impunity" the man he believes has injured him. It is also the story of a sick, maniacal mind. The action of the story is the acting out of his, Montresor's, revenge as he lures a man named Fortunato to a wine cellar where he seals him in a wall to die. We have no lesson here, but we learn about the force of revenge and about the state of the mind obsessed with it.

That example was easy. Now read the opening of Cheever's *The Country Husband.*

To begin at the beginning, the airplane from Minneapolis in which Francis Weed was traveling East ran into heavy weather. The sky had been a hazy blue, with the clouds below the plane lying so close together that nothing could be seen of the earth. Then mist began to form outside the windows, and they flew into a white cloud of such density that it reflected the exhaust fires. The color of the cloud darkened to gray, and the plane began to rock. Francis had been in heavy weather before, but he had never been shaken up so much. The man in the seat beside him pulled a flask out of his pocket and took a drink. Francis smiled at his neighbor, but the man looked away; he wasn't sharing his painkiller with anyone. The plane had begun to drop and flounder wildly. A child was crying. The air in the cabin was overheated and stale, and Francis' left foot went to sleep. He read a little from a paper book that he had bought at the airport, but the violence of the storm divided his attention. It was black outside the ports. The exhaust fires blazed and shed sparks in the dark, and, inside, the shaded lights, the stuffiness, and the window curtains gave the cabin an atmosphere of intense and misplaced domesticity. Then the light flickered and went out. "You know what I've always wanted to do?" the man beside Francis said suddenly. "I've always wanted to buy a farm in New Hampshire and raise beef cattle." The stewardess announced that they were going to make an emergency landing. All but the child saw in their minds the spreading wings of the Angel of Death. The pilot could be heard singing faintly, "I've got sixpence, jolly, jolly sixpence. I've got sixpence to last me all my life . . ." There was no other sound.

This one may be tougher, but you still ask yourself the same question: What do you expect the rest of the story to be about? You might answer, "The events surrounding the plane's landing: the crash, the rescue effort, and maybe the bonding of the victims as they rely on each other for survival."

Perhaps you then set up a hypothesis of theme that goes something like this: This will probably be a story about life and death, about how death is always waiting at the next corner, and about how people behave and relate to one another in a crisis. When you go on to read the next few paragraphs, you may be surprised to discover that the people on the plane all walk away from the crash and that the main character simply goes home.

Your expectations of plot were wrong, but was your hypothesis of the theme wrong as well? Are there still ways in which the story is about how death is waiting and about how people behave and relate to other people in a crisis? This is ultimately a story about midlife crisis, about how a man's brush with death, which forces him to realize that he won't live forever, makes him reconsider his life. He has to ask himself if he's living the life he wants. He behaves erratically and struggles through this crisis, but finally settles back into a routine, the midlife crisis ending as many do: Francis Weed adjusts to the life he has made for himself. We understand more about middle age after reading this story, but we have been given no easy moral. Not until false hypotheses are dispensed with and all the events of the story are pondered, can you arrive at conclusions about theme.

Exercise

The Country Husband is episodic; it develops in a series of scenes in which Francis Weed's actions and thoughts are central. Analyze this story scene by scene, looking for suggestions of theme or a dominant impression in each and listing these suggestions below. When you have finished, consider any patterns you see that give you an overview of the story and that lead you to an interpretation of its major theme. State this theme. List any minor themes. Let the explanation of this story given above help you to focus your thoughts.

SCENE	SUGGESTED THEME OR DOMINANT IMPRESSION
Example: Francis's arrival home	*War: living room is "divided like Gaul into three parts"; "children are absorbed in own antagonisms"; the mother's call to dinner is "like the war cries of the Scottish chieftains"; the household reflects the war Francis is having with himself*

His encounter with the
  maid at the party

His ride home with the
  babysitter

His train ride to work

His conversation with
  Gertrude

His conversation with
  Clayton

His fight with Julia

His conversation with Trace

His arrival at the
  psychiatrist's office

His evening of
  woodworking

MAJOR THEME:

MINOR THEMES:

The process of discovering theme is essentially one of remaining alert as you read, of thinking about what you are reading, and of attempting to interpret the literature as you go along. Only when you have completed your reading can you move toward some final considerations of theme by putting together all your thoughts and seeing where they lead and where they do not. Just as your perspective on a person changes as you get to know him or her, your understanding of a work of literature develops as you become more familiar with it. You must be patient with a complex work of literature, assessing its theme as you go along, but reserving final judgment until you know enough not to be fooled by first impressions.

Exercise

1. Read section I of Keats's "To Autumn." It is obviously a poem about autumn, but *what* about autumn? What is its theme? Look for patterns in the words in section I. Are any ideas repeated? What hypothesis(es) for themes do these patterns suggest? How is this theme developed in the subsequent sections?
2. Read Abraham's opening speech in *The Sacrifice of Isaac*. What is its main concern? What do we learn about the man Abraham, his life, circumstances, and values? What possible theme or themes for the play do your answers suggest? Read the play to test your hypothesis(es).
3. After reading *Young Goodman Brown*, reread the final section from the point at which Goodman Brown wakes in the morning. How does this closing focus the reader's attention on theme? What passages from this section are particularly significant in a consideration of theme? Why aren't we told whether or not he was dreaming? Why are we told what is carved on his tombstone?

RELATING DETAILS TO THEME

Whether the details in the work you are studying form a plot line, as with most short stories and plays and some narrative poems, or not, as with most poems, you must in your essay relate these details to the major theme of the work. Since organizing the details of an action line is different from organizing the details of a progression of images or ideas, let's look at the two processes separately.

Organizing the Details of a
Plot Line and Writing the Draft

The discussion of plot in your textbook describes the five parts of a narrative action line: exposition, rising action, climax, falling action, and conclusion or catastrophe. In organizing your paper, you may wish, for convenience, to combine discussions of some of these parts, depending upon the emphasis you will be giving to each. The first part might include the exposition or introduction of the characters and situation and the rising action in which the conflicts and complications of the story build. The second part of your summary might focus only on the climax, the point in the action at which something crucial happens, something that will determine the outcome of the story. The third part might contain the falling action and the conclusion, during which the reader witnesses the aftermath of the climax and discovers its significance through its influence on the outcome. These three parts would essentially correspond to the paragraphs of the body of your summary. In each paragraph in the body of your essay, you condense and describe what occurs in a single phase of the story (that's the summary part) and relate the action to the work's theme (that's the interpretive part).

Relating the action to the theme will most often be a matter of interpreting the events in these five parts in terms of the central character and his or her actions. Remember the narrator in *The Cask of Amontillado;* he is also the central character. Review the exposition in the first paragraph, which we earlier said indicated the theme of revenge. The action line throughout traces the central character on his journey of revenge. If you have trouble recognizing these segments of action, look for them as they occur in the movements of the main character. If it makes your work any easier, imagine that you are watching a television production of the story. Where would the commercials most comfortably fit? Are these points the legitimate breaks in the action?

Exercise

Follow the movements of the main characters in these works of literature and describe briefly what occurs in each of the parts of the line of action.

1. Abraham in *The Sacrifice of Isaac*
2. La Folle in *Beyond the Bayou*
3. Mr. Flood in "Mr. Flood's Party"
4. Prufrock in "The Love Song of J. Alfred Prufrock"

Writing the draft of your summary is largely a matter of determining where the segments of action begin and end or where one image or group of images (in a nonnarrative work) begins and ends so you can decide what will be contained in the paragraphs of the body and how many of these paragraphs there will be. Your introduction will be like any other. You will (1) attract the audience's attention in some provocative way; (2) state your central idea (which in this case is to say that the plot of the piece of narrative literature reflects a theme, which you then name); and (3) provide some indication of your essay's method of procedure.

Working from the basic essay outline form given below, good for any kind of paper anywhere, follow the steps used in preparing this draft of a summary of *The Cask of Amontillado*.

OUTLINE
Title
Introduction
    Opening
    Central idea
    Statement of procedure

Body
  Topic sentence
    Detailed sentences
  Next topic sentence
    Detailed sentences
  Other topic sentences,with details, as needed
Conclusion
  Final synthesis
  Snappy closing

Your opening should, first and foremost, interest the reader in your paper. The central idea statement explains the main point and purpose of your paper. Since the main point of an interpretive summary is to relate the action line or images to the theme, your central idea must include this theme. Your statement of procedure then can make a preliminary statement about how the action of the story (and thus the paragraphs of your paper) will be broken down. Here is the opening paragraph of an interpretive summary of *The Cask of Amontillado.*

An Interpretive Summary of The Cask of
              Amontillado

   In Edgar Allan Poe's short story The
Cask of Amontillado, the seemingly mad and
fanatical Montresor executes his revenge of
some unnamed insult against his supposed
enemy Fortunato. The action of the story is
the narrator's slow luring of his enemy to
his doom and his savoring of Fortunato's
slowly dawning horror at realizing his fate.

Now look at how the student broke the action down as you read the first paragraph of the body of her essay. Note particularly how she is summarizing this action to show *how it develops theme.* Thus the idea of revenge is integral to her paragraph, to the topic sentence and detail sentences.

First
paragraph of
the body
will explain
first
segment
of action.
Theme
stated in
topic
sentence.

As the story opens, the main characters meet at a carnival where Montresor initiates his plot of revenge by asking Fortunato, a connoisseur of wines, to judge whether or not a cask of wine he bought is the prized Amontillado wine. To ensure that Fortunato will "take the bait," fall into his scheme of revenge, Montresor pricks his vanity by implying that Luchresi, another wine taster, would do as well. Fortunato, fittingly dressed as a court jester or fool for the carnival, is offended: "Luchresi cannot tell Amontillado from Sherry." He urges Montresor to take him to his wine cellar immediately.

Here the exposition has been summarized. We know who the characters are, what the problem is, and we are ready for real action to occur. Read the student's next paragraph.

Next
segment of
action
begins.
Theme is
again
reiterated.

Upon their arrival at Montresor's house, there are hints that evil lurks, that Montresor's revenge has been carefully planned. He has made sure the house is empty, and he is overly generous in plying Fortunato with wine, "Medoc against the damp." We watch as Montresor leads the drunken Fortunato further and deeper into the catacombs, damp stifling chambers of death with a "foulness of air." This foreboding journey continues until Montresor leads Fortunato into a dark crypt by

```
a pile of bones where the Amontil-
lado is supposedly stored. But Fortunato
discovers there is none there.
```

Thus ends the next segment of action, the long, suspenseful segment of rising action. There is suddenly a turn in the action, a point at which Fortunato realizes his fate and a point at which a tense audience might scream. We're beginning an unusually long climax.

```
    Montresor begins to find his revenge as he
suddenly chains Fortunato against the wall
of a niche. He savors the moment as Fortunato
begins to realize his fate, that Montresor is
going to wall him in. When Fortunato rattles
his chains in horror, Montresor stops his
work to hear this music to his maniacal ears.
As Fortunato yells in defiance and incredulity,
Montresor "surpasses [the yells] in volume and
strength . . . until the clamor" and the
climax end.
```

See now how the student combines her summary of the falling action with her conclusion.

```
    In the dreadful calm that follows this
"clamor," Montresor reaches the pinnacle he
hoped for in the story's first paragraph.
"I must not only punish, but punish with
impunity." After Fortunato cannot cajole
him out of his plan, he pleads, "For the love
of God" only to have the madman reply, "Yes,
```

```
for the love of God," and seal the last brick
in place and pile the bones in front. Here is
punishment indeed. And there is impunity in
this story of evil revenge, for Montresor
tells us that for a "half century no mortal
has disturbed that pile of bones" and dis-
covered his evil deed. He has committed the
perfect crime!
```

- The theme of the work of literature is your paper's unifying factor. Notice the frequent repetition of the word "revenge."
- The structure of the work of literature will suggest the structure of your essay.
- The details in your paragraphs are derived from the work of literature but are interpreted by you.
- An accurate interpretive summary includes a description of the segments of action (or series of images) in a work and an explanation of *how they develop theme.*

Exercise

1. Where is the climax in each of the following narrative works? If you can identify it, you should be able to see how the other segments of action relate to it.
   "My Last Duchess"
   Young Goodman Brown
   Araby
   "Mr. Flood's Party"
   The Sacrifice of Isaac
2. Often students are asked to write a one-paragraph summary of a work as part of a larger assignment. Practice by writing a one-paragraph summary of *The Cask of Amontillado.* Write a one-sentence summary.

Organizing the Details of a Nonnarrative Work

Many poems and some stories and plays do not have plots. Instead, they may give impressions, pose ideas, build images. Such works do not have a convenient three- or five-part, built-in structure for you to use as a basis for organizing your essay. Instead, you need to look for patterns that develop within the work of literature and to recognize the organization the author has established. Only then will you be able to see the breaks or shifts in the progression of thought that will suggest how to structure the paragraphs of your summary.

Perhaps the best way to explain how to determine what are the "parts" of the thought line or image line of a poem is by example. Carefully read the following poem, "Southern Gothic," by Donald Justice.

SOUTHERN GOTHIC

(for W.E.B. & P.R.)

Something of how the homing bee at dusk
Seems to inquire, perplexed, how there can be
No flowers here, not even withered stalks of flowers,
Conjures a garden where no garden is
And trellises too frail almost to bear
The memory of a rose, much less a rose.
Great oaks, more monumentally great oaks now
Than ever when the living rose was new,
Cast shade that is the more completely shade
Upon a house of broken windows merely
And empty nests up under broken eaves.
No damask any more prevents the moon,
But it unravels, peeling from a wall,
Red roses within roses within roses.

There are no stanza breaks or rhyme patterns to guide you, so you must consider the poem in sentences and in shifts of thought. There is one central theme, the expression of which expands throughout the "sections" of the poem. What is this theme? What are these sections? How does a reader find them? First, look at the title. Remember that a good title should at least suggest an idea or image important to the understanding of theme. What does the phrase "Southern gothic" mean? Have you ever heard the expression before? If not, do you know what gothic means? In literature, gothic refers to a writing style that emphasizes the mysterious, the grotesque, and the desolate. The title, then, suggests that we will read about some grotesque, mysterious desolation of the South. Keeping in mind the thematic suggestions of the title, read the poem sentence by sentence to formulate and test a hypothesis.

What is your hypothesis after reading the first sentence? What kind of bee is it? What does he seem surprised to discover? As the speaker watches the bee's activities, what effect do they have on him?

A "homing" bee—not a wanderer, but an insect returning to a place where home should be—seems confused that the flowers are all gone. Watching this causes the speaker to envision a fragile garden with a trellis too frail to bear a rose, or even the memory of a rose, the rose to which the bee is returning. From this image alone, what hypotheses of theme might you develop? One would be that this is a poem about remembrances of things past. Recalling the title and its mention of the South, your mind begins to connect the two, and you realize that you are reading about the South that is "gone with the wind," about that opulent but fragile way of life before the Civil War, a life that was centered on the plantation that now is faded but not gone. Look at the next image to see how it develops this theme. "Great oaks" case a symbolic shadow on this broken house. This shadow is perhaps the shadow of ruin and decay. It is cast, ironically, by trees that were small and weak when the South was great, when its "rose" was on the vine. But now these trees are strong and tall and able to cast a pall on this house, this remnant of the past.

The house, in the next image, is described in a manner consistent with this developing hypothesis of theme. It has broken windows. It is decayed and ruined. The broken eaves have empty nests. No new generation takes up this way of life. All seems gone, over, finished.

In the next image, although there are no fine damask curtains at the windows of the ruined house and so the moon shows us the peeling wallpaper inside, we see "roses within roses within roses." A whole paragraph might be necessary to explain the symbolic suggestions of this closing image. But essentially this image shows that beauty persists within this decay; a charm still lingers in a haunting, gothic way.

An interpretive summary of a nonnarrative poem is an explication or clarification of images. You cannot condense what happens, since nothing necessarily does actually *happen*. So you must interpret the ideas and images. You may need a paragraph per image, or you may need to combine the discussion of two or more images in one paragraph. You must use your judgment about organizing this essay the same as you would with any essay.

Notice that while summaries of narrative (action-line) works usually condense the original, an explication-style summary will often be longer than the original work.

Exercise

Review the following poems. Which have plot lines with characters whose actions suggest organizing your summary around exposition, rising action, climax, falling action, and conclusion? Which have simply a progression of images?

1. "Let Me Not to the Marriage of True Minds"
2. "To an Athlete Dying Young"
3. "London"
4. "Dover Beach"
5. "Pied Beauty"
6. "The Rose Family"
7. "My Papa's Waltz"
8. "Sir Patrick Spens"

Select one of the poems to work with. Read it carefully and develop an hypothesis of theme. Then identify the parts of its line of action or its various images. Explain briefly how each part of the line of action or how each image develops the theme you have discovered in the poem. To help you with your work, review the following explication of Donald Justice's "Southern Gothic."

"Southern Gothic": An
Explanatory Summary

Donald Justice's "Southern Gothic" gives a
view of the haunting beauty that persists in
a grand Southern house despite its decay and
the ruin of the way of life it represents.
The very title itself prepares us for a look
at something grotesque and mysterious as we
come upon this gothic scene of a dilapidated
house left over from the South that flourished
before the Civil War. As we trace the various
images in the poem and the symbol of the rose,
which links them, we see this theme of beauty
in desolation slowly evolve.

The first image of this haunting beauty is
of a bee returning at dusk to find nothing
where a garden evidently once had been. He
is a "homing" bee who is "perplexed" to find
there are no more flowers for him here. The
speaker proclaims that watching this bee
search causes him to envision this former
garden, to envision fragile rose trellises.
They are, like the old days they depict, too
frail to bear the weight of even "the
memory of a rose." The fragile beauty of
this bygone era persists in such imaginings.

In the next image, we see the reality of
what has replaced the beauty of this time of
the rose trellis, namely, "great oaks." They
are larger now and stronger now than when
the "living rose was new." In their strength,
the strength of an age that has supplanted
the age of the genteel, opulent Old South,
they "cast shade that is the more completely
shade." Their shade falls on the house that,
like its time, is in ruin with "broken windows,"
"broken eaves," and "empty nests," with no
living youth to carry on.

However, in the closing image we see that all
that was truly beautiful from that past is not
entirely gone. In the desolation of persisting

beauty, as the moonlight falls on the interior
walls (since a house in ruin no longer has
fine damask curtains to prevent the light),
the peeling wallpaper reveals "red roses
within roses within roses." Despite what
time and circumstances have done to try to
strip this place of its beauty, this beauty--
like the layers of rose wallpaper--goes too
deep. It cannot all be peeled away. A haunting
beauty persists in the desolation.

Exercise

1. Are there any ideas or images crucial to the discussion
   that this essay failed to develop?
2. What key terms from the introduction of the essay are repeated throughout?
3. What transitions are used to connect paragraphs? to connect sentences within paragraphs?
4. Is the ending effective? Why or why not?

Analyzing Literature

3

An essay of literary analysis is probably the paper that will give you the greatest sense of accomplishment and satisfaction. By the time you finish it, you will know the story or play or poem so well you will feel as if you own it.

In analyzing literature, you look carefully at a particular characteristic (or several characteristics) of a work and explain how it contributes to the overall effect. You might analyze, for example, character, diction, irony, or symbol. Your analysis will help you to appreciate the skill and craft of the artist and, like any other close study of a work of literature, your analysis will lead you to a fuller, deeper, more rewarding understanding of and response to a work. Whether you recognize it or not, you encounter this kind of analytical study all the time, both inside and outside an academic setting. When you look at a painting and notice the color, thickness, and texture of the paint or the arrangement of the figures on the canvas, you are involving yourself in the business of analysis. Likewise, when your swimming coach watches your stroke, the extension of your arms, the movement of your legs, and the timing of the turning of your head as you come up for air, he is engaging in technical analysis. The more you know about painting or swimming as a skill, the fuller your appreciation of it as an art. When you look really closely and see all that goes into the execution of an artistic presentation, you are more likely to be struck by the magic of all the parts coming together to produce something beautiful.

Most of the papers you write for a literature course will be essays of analysis. You will be discussing how the artist has used his craft to put a poem or story or play together in order to create a work of art. You will be explaining how the whole point or theme of the work is reflected in the individual characteristics.

Exercise

1. As a group, select a sports figure, dancer, singer, or any other performing artist. Be sure that every group member knows this artist and agrees that the artist is good at what he or she does. Now analyze what contributes to that effect. What characteristics make that artist's performance so good? *How* do they make it so good?
2. Select a work of literature you have already discussed in class. Identify its theme. Discuss specific characteristics in terms of *how* they reflect this theme.
3. Write a one-paragraph summary of your conclusions.

To write a coherent and effective technical analysis essay, you will need to be organized in your efforts. A reasonable procedure would include these steps:
1. searching for a topic
2. establishing a thesis
3. gathering textual evidence
4. developing valid inferences
5. designing the outline
6. developing the draft.

Let us consider what is involved in each of the steps listed above so that you can make efficient use of your time once you start your work and so that you will meet as few frustrations as possible.

SEARCHING FOR A TOPIC

Perhaps your instructor will give you a specific assignment, such as "write about situation and setting in Leonard Cohen's 'Suzanne Takes You Down,'" eliminating the need for you to search for a topic. Be grateful—this will save you a good bit of time.

But frequently, an assignment is not nearly so specific. You might be asked to write about a characteristic of your choosing in a work of literature that the teacher has selected. Or you might be asked to write about, say, imagery in some work of your own choosing. You might even be sent out entirely on your own to determine what feature of what work of literature you are going to write about. Choosing the right topic for yourself and for your skills and interests could make all the difference in how much you enjoy the assignment, how easy you find it to accomplish, and how well you succeed.

If your instructor has assigned a specific work of literature, but not the technical device you must analyze, you might decide what feature to analyze in one of these two ways. Begin reading or rereading the assignment and stop the first time you find yourself noticing some characteristic of the literature. For example, as you begin reading the opening of a play in which the playwright is setting the stage for the first scene, you find yourself thinking, "Red sky? I wonder why he wants a red sky above the buildings in the backdrop." Continue to read with an eye to all references to light and color. Are they used to reflect mood? enhance theme? What is significant about the way color is used? *Let your topic find you by being alert to your reactions to what you read.*

Or is there one characteristic—setting, symbol, figurative language—that you have recognized and understood more easily than others as you have read other works of literature? Perhaps it would make for a good topic here. Learn to recognize your talents and use them to your advantage. But never turn away from the challenge of writing about a trait that you do not easily understand. Writing an analysis can teach you what you need to know; it can help to strengthen your weak skills.

You might also take a clue from the authors of your text, who have placed many of the works under specific topics of study, making obvious suggestions for analysis. If a short story has been placed under "setting" in the table of contents, you can be sure that the setting is rich with detail waiting to be analyzed. But don't be afraid to analyze that same story for character or focus.

Exercise

1. No work of literature is composed of plot, speaker, or symbol alone. Every work of literature uses many technical devices. Why do you suppose that the authors of your text placed Nathaniel Hawthorne's *Young Goodman Brown* under the heading of "Symbol"? Why might they have placed Emily Dickinson's "After Great Pain" under "Words"?
2. Read several poems from the "Poems for Further Reading" section of your textbook. If you had to place each under some other headings in the poetry section of the table of contents, what headings would they be? Discuss your reasons.
3. Select a play from the text, perhaps one the class has already read and discussed. If you were to use headings for drama like those in the fiction section, where would you place the play you have chosen? Why?

ESTABLISHING A THESIS

The thesis of any technical analysis is essentially: "This particular characteristic in this work of literature contributes to its theme and overall effect." The thesis may become more complex if you discuss more than one technical characteristic, or depending on the nature of your specific assignment, it may take on some certain slant. But any thesis for this kind of paper follows this standard form.

Before you can write your thesis statement, however, you must develop a statement of the theme of the work of literature, the idea or overall effect to which the technical device contributes. (You may want to review the "What Theme Is—and Is Not" and "Finding the Theme" sections in Chapter 2.) Imagine that you are working with Katherine Mansfield's "Her First Ball" and have concluded that this is a story whose theme is how the excitement of being young and carefree blocks out any gloomy suggestion that youth doesn't last for long. You have decided to analyze focus. Your thesis, following the standard form suggested above, would read like this: "Focus in Katherine Mansfield's *Her First Ball* contributes to the theme of how the excitement of being young and carefree blocks out any gloomy suggestion that youth doesn't last for long."

You should now ask yourself *how* focus contributes to theme and refine your thesis based on your answer. How does the focus help you to appreciate Leila's excitement? What types of detail does the story focus on? How would the story seem different if told from the point of view of the older man or of Leila's cousin? Your revised version might read this way: "Katherine Mansfield's use of limited omniscient focus helps the reader see, through the eyes of a young country girl thrilled at the prospect of her first city dance, how the excitement of being young and carefree blocks out any gloomy suggestion that youth doesn't last for long."

Such a thesis, as a part of your opening, will give your reader a clear sense of your purpose. And more importantly perhaps, at this stage of the composition, it will give you a strong sense of your essay's direction.

Exercise

Practice writing thesis statements for these paper topics.

1. Focus in *The Most Dangerous Game*

2. Focus and Voice in *Our Friend Judith*
3. Setting in *The Artificial Nigger*
4. Speaker in "My Last Duchess"
5. Sound in "Dirge"
6. Figurative Language in "To Autumn"
7. Symbolism in *The Glass Menagerie*

GATHERING EVIDENCE
FOR THE BODY OF YOUR ESSAY

Now that you have a thesis, you must set about gathering from the text the evidence that led you to your thesis. Textual evidence consists of direct references to events, ideas, descriptions, and actual passages from the work that you will use to support your thesis. The body of your essay is simply a well organized presentation of textual evidence accompanied by your own explanation of exactly *how* this material is evidence of what you say it is. A gun in a murder trial is worthless as a piece of "evidence" unless the prosecutor can link it to both the crime and the defendant. It is your job to link your evidence to the central action of the work you are writing about and ultimately to your thesis.

You gather evidence by rereading the work of literature several times and noting the passages that help you to develop the point of your essay. Take a pen or pencil and mark up your book. Underline key passages, circle significant words, write notes to yourself in the margin, or just make question marks if you are not yet sure what there is to say about the passage. Draw lines and arrows linking passages. It is likely that the more you read, the more you will notice and the more you will become aware of connections you had not even seen when you originally developed your thesis.

Here is a typical annotation of Wilfred Owen's "Dulce et Decorum Est" by a student preparing an analysis of the contribution of word choice and images to the theme that it is not sweet and proper to die for one's country in war.

Handwritten annotations (right margin, top to bottom): not dignified / no high status; dregs of society; not sweet language; not a proud march; no glorious uniforms; not a bold march; reduced to a scrambling panic; not sedate or refined; panic of drowning in gas; opposite of sweet snappy cadence call; no time to move him gently and with respect; horror of look on his face; disgusting physical images; no high zest in a real battle; speaker's vitality; of war is not glory at all

Handwritten annotations (left margin, top to bottom): unrefined; like trudge undignified walk; poet concentrating on physical appearances; speaker remembers this later; like a gassed soldier; "unsweet" destruction of his body; angry tone

Circled/marked words in text and inline notes: not dignified; disgusting; no glorious uniforms; Latin: foreign language and a foreign idea to the speaker

Bent double, like old beggars under sacks,
Knock-kneed, coughing like hags, we cursed through
    the sludge,
Till on the haunting flares we turned our backs
And towards our distant rest began to trudge.
Men marched asleep. Many had lost their boots
But limped on, blood-shod. All went lame; all blind;
Drunk with fatigue; deaf even to the hoots
Of disappointed shells that dropped behind.

Gas! Gas! Quick, boys—An ecstasy of fumbling,
Fitting the clumsy helmets just in time;
But someone still was yelling out and stumbling
And floundering like a man in fire or lime.—
Dim, through the misty panes and thick green light
As under a green sea, I saw him drowning.

In all my dreams, before my helpless sight,
He plunges at me, guttering, choking, drowning.

If in some smothering dream you too could pace
Behind the wagon that we flung him in,
And watch the white eyes writhing in his face,
His hanging face, like a devil's sick of sin;
If you could hear, at every jolt, the blood
Come gargling from the froth-corrupted lungs,
Obscene as cancer, bitter as the cud
Of vile, incurable sores on innocent tongues,—
My friend, you would not tell with such high zest
To children ardent for some desperate glory,
The old Lie: Dulce et decorum est
Pro patria mori.

This student now has the basics of his paper: a thesis, textual evidence, and commentary to link that evidence to the thesis. Some of these markings and comments may never find their way into the final essay. Moreover, as he writes his outline or his draft, the student may notice other significant words and ideas that he did not mark. He can always incorporate his new insights.

Can you find evidence that would further the thesis but that the student missed?

Exercise

1. Annotate this passage from Hawthorne's *Young Goodman Brown* for an analysis essay discussing the author's use of setting to enhance the theme of evil within us and of one man's loss of faith in God. Compare your notations with those of other members of the class. How similar or different are they?

> In truth, all through the haunted forest, there could be nothing more frightful than the figure of Goodman Brown. On he flew, among the black pines, brandishing his staff with frenzied gestures, now giving vent to an inspiration of horrid blasphemy, and now shouting forth such laughter, as set all the echoes of the forest laughing like demons around him. The fiend in his own shape is less hideous, than when he rages in the breast of man. Thus sped the demoniac on his course, until, quivering among the trees, he saw a red light before him, as when the felled trunks and branches of a clearing have been set on fire, and throw up their lurid blaze against the sky, at the hour of midnight. He paused, in a lull of the tempest that had driven him onward, and heard the swell of what seemed a hymn, rolling solemnly from a distance, with the weight of many voices. He knew the tune; it was a familiar one in the choir of the village meeting-house. The verse died heavily away, and was lengthened by a chorus, not of human voices, but of all the sounds of the benighted wilderness, pealing in awful harmony together. Goodman Brown cried out; and his cry was lost to his own ear, by its unison with the cry of the desert.

2. Annotate this passage from Oscar Wilde's *The Importance of Being Earnest* for an analysis demonstrating how the playwright has developed the character of Lady Bracknell to reflect his theme that the members of polite society in England at the turn of the century were shallow and interested only in appearances. Compare notes with your classmates.

> LADY BRACKNELL   Mr. Worthing! Rise, sir, from this semi-recumbent posture. It is most indecorous.
>
> GWENDOLEN   Mamma! [*He tries to rise; she restrains him.*] I must beg you to retire. This is no place for you. Besides, Mr. Worthing has not quite finished yet.
>
> LADY BRACKNELL   Finished what, may I ask?

GWENDOLEN   I am engaged to Mr. Worthing, mamma.

They rise together.

LADY BRACKNELL   Pardon me, you are not engaged to anyone. When you do become engaged to some one, I, or your father, should his health permit him, will inform you of the fact. An engagement should come on a young girl as a surprise, pleasant or unpleasant, as the case may be. It is hardly a matter that she could be allowed to arrange for herself. . . . And now I have a few questions to put to you, Mr. Worthing. While I am making these inquiries, you, Gwendolen, will wait for me below in the carriage.

GWENDOLEN [*reproachfully*]   Mamma!

LADY BRACKNELL   In the carriage, Gwendolen!

> GWENDOLEN *goes to the door. She and* JACK *blow kisses to each other behind* LADY BRACKNELL's *back.* LADY BRACKNELL *looks vaguely about as if she could not understand what the noise was. Finally turns around.*

Gwendolen, the carriage!

GWENDOLEN   Yes, mamma. [*Goes out, looking back at* JACK.]

LADY BRACKNELL [*sitting down*]   You can take a seat, Mr. Worthing. [*Looks in her pocket for notebook and pencil.*]

JACK   Thank you, Lady Bracknell, I prefer standing.

LADY BRACKNELL [*pencil and notebook in hand*]   I feel bound to tell you that you are not down on my list of eligible young men, although I have the same list as the dear Duchess of Bolton has. We work together, in fact. However, I am quite ready to enter your name, should your answers be what a really affectionate mother requires. Do you smoke?

JACK   Well, yes, I must admit I smoke.

LADY BRACKNELL   I am glad to hear it. A man should always have an occupation of some kind. There are far too many idle men in London as it is. How old are you?

JACK   Twenty-nine.

LADY BRACKNELL   A very good age to be married at. I have always been of the opinion that a man who desires to get married should know either everything or nothing. Which do you know?

JACK [*after some hesitation*]   I know nothing, Lady Bracknell.

LADY BRACKNELL   I am pleased to hear it. I do not approve of anything that tampers with natural ignorance. Ignorance is like a delicate exotic fruit; touch it and the bloom is gone. The whole theory of modern education is radically unsound. Fortunately in England, at any rate, education produces no effect whatsoever. If it did, it would prove a serious danger to the upper classes, and probably lead to acts of violence in Grosvenor Square. What is your income?

JACK   Between seven and eight thousand a year.

LADY BRACKNELL [*makes a note in her book*]   In land, or in investments?

JACK   In investments, chiefly.

LADY BRACKNELL   That is satisfactory. What between the duties expected of one during one's lifetime, and the duties exacted from one after one's death, land has ceased to be either a profit or a pleasure. It gives one position, and prevents one from keeping it up. That's all that can be said about land.

JACK   I have a country house with some land, of course, attached to it, about fifteen hundred acres, I believe; but I don't depend on that for my real income. In fact, as far as I can make out, the poachers are the only people who make anything out of it.

LADY BRACKNELL   A country house! How many bedrooms? Well, that point can be cleared up afterwards. You have a town house, I hope? A girl with a simple, unspoiled nature, like Gwendolen, could hardly be expected to reside in the country.

JACK   Well, I own a house in Belgrave Square, but it is let by the year to Lady Bloxham. Of course, I can get it back whenever I like, at six months' notice.

LADY BRACKNELL   Lady Bloxham? I don't know her.

JACK   Oh, she goes about very little. She is a lady considerably advanced in years.

LADY BRACKNELL   Ah, nowadays that is no guarantee of respectability of character. What number in Belgrave Square?

JACK   149.

LADY BRACKNELL [*shaking her head*]   The unfashionable side. I thought there was something. However, that could easily be altered.

JACK   Do you mean the fashion, or the side?

LADY BRACKNELL [*sternly*]   Both, if necessary, I presume. What are your politics?

JACK   Well, I am afraid I really have none. I am a Liberal Unionist.

LADY BRACKNELL   Oh, they count as Tories. They dine with us. Or come in the evening, at any rate. Now to minor matters. Are your parents living?

JACK   I have lost both my parents.

LADY BRACKNELL   To lose one parent, Mr. Worthing, may be regarded as a misfortune; to lose both looks like carelessness. Who was your father? He was evidently a man of some wealth. Was he born in what the Radical papers call the purple of commerce, or did he rise from the ranks of the aristocracy?

JACK   I am afraid I really don't know. That fact is, Lady Bracknell, I said I had lost my parents. It would be nearer the truth to say that my parents seem to have lost me. . . . I don't actually know who I am by birth. I was . . . well, I was found.

LADY BRACKNELL   Found!

JACK   The late Mr. Thomas Cardew, an old gentleman of a very charitable and kindly disposition, found me, and gave me the name of Worthing, because he happened to have a first-class ticket for Worthing in his pocket at the time. Worthing is a place in Sussex. It is a seaside resort.

LADY BRACKNELL   Where did the charitable gentleman who had a first-class ticket for this seaside resort find you?

JACK [*gravely*]   In a handbag.

LADY BRACKNELL   A handbag?

JACK [*very seriously*]   Yes, Lady Bracknell. I was in a handbag—a somewhat large, black leather handbag, with handles to it—an ordinary handbag in fact.

LADY BRACKNELL   In what locality did this Mr. James, or Thomas, Cardew come across this ordinary handbag?

JACK   In the cloakroom at Victoria Station. It was given to him in mistake for his own.

LADY BRACKNELL   The cloakroom at Victoria Station?

JACK   Yes. The Brighton line.

LADY BRACKNELL   The line is immaterial. Mr. Worthing, I confess I feel somewhat bewildered by what you have just told me. To be born, or at any rate bred, in a handbag, whether it had handles or not, seems to me to display a contempt for the ordinary decencies of family life that reminds one of the worst excesses of the French Revolution. And I presume you know what the unfortunate movement led to? As for the particular locality in which the handbag was found, a cloakroom at a railway station might serve to conceal a social indiscretion—has probably, indeed, been used for that purpose before now—but it could hardly be regarded as an assured basis for a recognized position in good society.

JACK   May I ask you then what you would advise me to do? I need hardly say I would do anything in the world to ensure Gwendolen's happiness.

LADY BRACKNELL   I would strongly advise you, Mr. Worthing, to try and acquire some relations as soon as possible, and to make a definite effort to produce at any rate one parent, of either sex, before the season is quite over.

JACK   Well, I don't see how I could possibly manage to do that. I can produce the handbag at any moment. It is in my dressing-room at home. I really think that should satisfy you, Lady Bracknell.

LADY BRACKNELL   Me, sir! What has it to do with me? You can hardly imagine that I and Lord Bracknell would dream of allowing our only daughter—a girl brought up with the utmost care—to marry into a cloakroom, and form an alliance with a parcel. Good morning, Mr. Worthing!

DEVELOPING VALID INFERENCES

Now that you have gathered textual evidence in support of your thesis, you must explain its significance. Without your commentary on its significance, your paper will not show *how* the characteristic you are analyzing reflects the theme of the literature. Your explanation will depend on logical inferences that you draw from the textual evidence. How effective you are will depend on how reasonable your conclusions seem, which in turn will depend upon the quality and weight of your evidence and the logic of your reasoning.

Suppose you are making the point that Wilfred Owen's poem, "Dulce et Decorum Est," advances the idea that war is not sweet and dignified by using carefully designed images of soliders at the front coming under a gas attack, images that are intended to horrify and sicken the reader. First, look at the quality of the textual evidence. Many words and phrases suggest ugliness and wretchedness. They do not connote other ideas equally emphatically, and they are not countered by a host of other words and phrases suggesting sweetness and dignity or indeed any other positive qualities. There is a conspicuous absence of any images suggesting that war is good or glorious. Notice that many of the passages marked during the reading of the poem become the pieces of evidence the student will discuss in the body of his essay to persuade the reader that the poem's words and images develop a theme of the vileness of war. "Stumbling," "floundering," "guttering," "choking," "writhing," "blood-shod," "froth-corrupted," and others are examples of the wretchedness of these soldiers.

Second, look at the weight of the evidence. Does it tip the scales in favor of your thesis? Notice that these images carry all the way through the poem. Ugliness appears early on, is consistently developed throughout, and rings through the closing idea. When you write an analysis, you need to convince yourself as you select a topic and convince the reader as you write the paper of the validity of your observations with the preponderance of your evidence. If the work of literature is indeed a good one, finding the evidence should not be too difficult for the conscientious reader.

If there is evidence that appears to contradict your thesis, you must be careful not to ignore it, but to explain it. How do you account for these seeming contradictions? Is the narrator's thought evolving? Is he gradually changing his position on an issue? Is the contradictory material an opposing point of view that the literature also examines? Is there an ironic statement a reader might mistake at face value? Is the situation a paradox where seeming contradictions live side by side? Resolve whatever confusion contradictory evidence might breed.

Third, look at your reasoning process. Will a reader be able to see your logic? Have you avoided oversimplification and faulty generalizations? Have you ignored any evidence? Consider the logical inadequacies in the reasoning that might have led to this statement: "Wilfred Owen's poem 'Dulce et Decorum Est' describes the march of a group of shameful soldiers who are a disgrace and a mockery of the idea of the true and noble warrior." Suppose the writer of this statement used as evidence the fact that the soldiers are said to be "beggars," "hags," that they are described as "drunk," "fumbling," and "clumsy." Suppose the writer says that one of the soliders is described as "stumbling" and as having a face "like a devil's." Taken by themselves, these words seem harsh indictments.

Such oversimplification results from taking these words out of context. No word, phrase, or even whole sentence in a piece of literature has the same meaning in isolation that it will have when read in the context of the entire work. The soldiers are only "like beggars under sacks" because they are disheveled by the hardship of their march and bent with the weight of their packs on weary shoulders. They are "coughing like hags" because they are sick, probably from living outside for a long time without enough food and sleep. They are not truly drunk, but "drunk with fatigue." And when the gas attack comes, they are "fumbling" for helmets that are "clumsy" to handle in the panic of trying to position their gas masks in time. One is indeed "stumbling," but it is because the gas has penetrated his lungs. His face is like a "devil's, sick of sin." The ravages of war and particularly of this gas attack are so horrible, the poet suggests, that even the devil, who loves evil, would have had enough.

The generalizations in the original statement then are faulty, not based on complete evidence. And the incompleteness of the evidence shows that the writer has ignored much that is in the text of the poem.

Your inferences must be drawn from complete evidence taken in context and with consideration of the entire work of literature.

Exercise

What valid inferences can be drawn from the passages you marked in *Young Goodman Brown* and *The Importance of Being Earnest*? Discuss.

DESIGNING THE OUTLINE

Using an outline will help you to make sure that you have touched on all important points before you begin the actual writing, and it will present you with an opportunity to organize your thoughts ahead of time to ensure the most coherent presentation possible. It may not be necessary for you to bother with a formal outline, but you should determine what the main sections of your essay will be and what points or evidence will go into each one. In general, the more you think, plan, and write about your subject, the more you will learn. You will find new evidence, have new insights about the evidence, and discover new and better ways to develop your ideas.

Consider the parts or sections of the essay abstractly first.

Part 1:   INTRODUCTION (probably one paragraph long)
• opening
• thesis (a statement in which you explain that you will dis-

cuss how the artist uses a certain technique to promote a
certain theme)
• statement of procedure (some indication of the direction
  and organization of your essay)
Part 2:   BODY (as many paragraphs as required by your evidence)

(Sample paragraph outline)

• topic sentence (reiterates the thesis by introducing your
  first unit of evidence)
• detail sentence ideas (composed of examples of evidence
  and your commentary linking it to the thesis)
• and so on
Part 3:   CONCLUSION (probably one paragraph long)
• summary, if necessary
• final note that reinforces thesis and sounds an ending

Here is the successful outline for a paper on Owen's powerful use of word choice to create effective images in the
poem we have been discussing.

```
Part 1: INTRODUCTION
. opening: Latin phrase "Dulce . . ." with
  translation
• thesis: Owen made powerful use of words to
  create images that show how ugly dying in
  war really is.
• statement of procedure: The paper will
  analyze the poet's physical description of
  soldiers on a march.
Part 2: BODY
• paragraph on how terrible the soldiers look
  even as they march along before the gas
  attack
  • "bent-double"--look weary and stooped
  • "beggars"--like the dregs of society
    rather than gleaming heroes
  • "coughing"--sickly
  • "hags"--ugly, worn
  • "trudge"--tired, laborious walking
  • "limped"--seem wounded or beaten down
```

- "blood-shod"--no shiny boots, just
  crusted blood
- "drunk w/fatigue"--bleary and weary
- paragraph on the horrors of the gas attack
  - "fumbling"--lose control in their panic
  - "clumsy helmets"--adds to the horror when
    helmets won't go on
  - "yelling"--more scenes of horror, not glory,
    in battle
  - "floundering"--flailing man seems weak and
    helpless--not a sweet picture
  - "stumbling"--weak and helpless again
  - "drowning"--dying horribly before their
    eyes
- paragraph about the ugly effect of the gas
  on one man and the philosophy to which it
  leads the speaker
  - "guttering"--throat is eaten away by
    the gas
  - "white eyes writhing"--ugly view of an
    honorable death
  - "face hanging"--horrible effects of gas on
    an already weary soldier
  - "blood . . . gargling"--concrete images
    of the destruction of his insides
  - "froth-corrupted lungs"--forces us to see
    the agony of the suffering of the body
  - "incurable sores"--disgusting, not
    glorious
  - "Dulce . . ."--is indeed a lie

Part 3: CONCLUSION: Latin phrase reinforced.

Exercise

Develop an outline from one of the thesis statements you
prepared for the exercise in the first part of this chapter on
page 61.

Does working on the outline cause you to reconsider and
revise your thesis statement? In what way or ways?

Is your evidence consistent? complete? Do any parts of
the text seem to clash with your thesis? How can you recon-
cile them?

WRITING THE DRAFT

Preparing the draft of the essay from such an outline should require no new skill on your part, nothing in addition to skills you learned in basic composition. In fact, a discussion of developing the draft appears here only to remind you to use good basic essay form in your technical analysis.

Remember that you should have:

- a clearly stated thesis
- paragraph topic sentences that advance the thesis by narrowing it to a particular discussion
- detail sentences that concretely develop the topic sentence
- a forceful closing that reiterates your thesis and strikes a note of finality.

Remember also that your essay is not tied to your outline so tightly that changes cannot be made. If you see an opportunity for improvement, take it.

Now take a look at the essay developed from the outline in the previous section.

An Analysis of Words and Images in "Dulce et
Decorum Eşt"

<u>Dulce et decorum est pro patria mori</u>.
It is sweet and proper to die for one's
country.

attention getting opening

This old saying is a lie, according to
Wilfred Owen in his poem, "Dulce et
Decorum Est." The poem suggests that
dying for one's country in war is certainly
ugly and horrible to watch. The poem
uses powerful descriptive words to create
images that show this horror. The impact
of the images and the connotations of
the words of the speaker reinforce the
theme as they show an awful gas attack
on a group of war-weary soldiers on the
march.

thesis

plan of procedure

topic sentence echoes essay's thesis and poem's theme

In the first section of the poem, even before the frightful gas attack begins, Owen uses his forceful language to show us a weary band of soldiers. By concentrating on their physical appearance, he lets us see war's devastating effect on the men. They are not gloriously gleaming soldiers proudly strutting, but are "bent double, like old beggars" and are "coughing like hags." They "trudge" through the elements, moving with difficulty, not at all boldly marching to battle. They have no wonderful bright uniforms or shiny boots, but are "blood-shod," their feet battered and crusted over in the terrible march. They are not any longer the finest physical specimens society has to offer, for they are "lame," "blind," and "deaf" to the sounds around them, "drunk with fatigue."

specific examples are fused with commentary

topic sentence echoes essay's thesis and poem's theme

As the gas attack begins in the next section of the poem, Owen gives us more words and images to ponder, more examples of the 'unsweetness' of the destruction of war. He shows us the ugliness of humans reduced to the indignities of a scrambling panic as the soldiers try to escape the poison behind the safety of their masks. Everyone is "fumbling" with the "clumsy helmets." One unsuccessful soldier is shown in agony, "yelling," "stumbling," "floundering" as he seems to drown, horribly, miserably in a sea of green gas.

specific examples are fused with commentary

topic sentence advances thesis as it echoes theme

The description is suddenly more graphic, uglier as Owen forces us to witness a dreadful kind of death as the gas destroys the lungs of the unfortunate soldier. The speaker remembers him "guttering, choking," as he rode in the wagon they had "flung him in." War provides no time for gentleness and human courtesy. The soldiers have to

toss him like a carcass and be on their way.
And as if it were not bad enough that his "white
eyes were writhing," every time the wagon hit
a bump, they could hear the blood "come gargling
from the froth-corrupted lungs." The gas was
eating his insides out. His lungs were corrupted as it indeed appears the dignity of
life is corrupted in this scene of war and
death.

specific examples are fused with commentary

Because the poet made the experience happen
for us as it did for the speaker in the poem
with his vivid language, it is not difficult
to understand how the speaker might conclude
in angry tones that someone having seen all
this could not tell the "lie": "<u>Dulce et
decorum est</u> / <u>Pro patria mori</u>."

reiteration of thesis

echoing of theme combined with forceful closing

The student organized this essay sequentially, as the evidence appeared in the poem. In this case, that pattern of organization was appropriate and effective.

What follows is an essay that does *not* organize evidence
in the same way at all. It discusses irony in Percy Bysshe
Shelly's "Ozymandias." The student analyzes various
kinds of ironies that are present in the general situation of
the poem. She organizes her essay around these types of
irony, not around any sequence of events in the poem.

Irony in "Ozymandias"

The central theme in Percy Bysshe Shelley's
poem "Ozymandias" is in itself an irony.
Ozymandias was a powerful Egyptian king
who was so certain that his power would last
that he had colossal statues with boastful
inscriptions sculpted. However powerful
Ozymandias was in his day, time has eroded
his reputation and his statues. Now the
proud inscriptions serve only to make a mockery
of the king who was so certain that his grandeur
would survive him. As the speaker in the
poem observes, "Nothing beside remains."

Shelley further develops this central ironic
theme by describing the ironic setting,
situations, and thoughts that surround this
"King of Kings," Ozymandias.

   The irony of the setting in which the
"traveler" finds Ozymandias emphasizes the
faded power and glory of the king. Instead
of being surrounded with a populated kingdom,
the "colossal wreck" rules over a "boundless
and bare" stretch of sand. The land to which
the decaying stones are bound forever is an
"antique land"--a land that has seen centuries
of history. Yet it is a desolate, sparsely
populated region, hardly befitting the
kingship of one who thought that he would
be timeless.

   Ozymandias's diminished power is reemphasized in the irony of the actual situations surrounding the ruins that the speaker
describes. There are huge fragments of what
once stood as a colossal statue, tall and
imposing and able to make its impression
seemingly throughout time. The fierce glare
of the statue's face, "the sneer of cold
command," must have evoked fear in all who
beheld it. What better way to assure the
faithfulness of his subjects than for
Ozymandias to have these features of strength
recorded for posterity in stone. Now, however,
the giant figure has been reduced to "truckless
legs of stone," disjointed from the head that
lies half-buried in the sand. The commanding
expression of the face no longer inspires
fear, but seems almost humorous. In fact, it
seems to heighten the irony that Ozymandias
is no longer a demanding reality, but is
instead a decaying one.

   Ozymandias himself ironically provides the
most convincing evidence that he survives
only as a crumbled memory when we read what
he thought of himself. The base of the
pedestal on which the magnificent representa-

tion once stood is inscribed with the words,
" 'My name is Ozymandias, King of Kings: /
Look on my works, ye Mighty, and despair!' "
But when we look on those works, we see only
lifeless wreckage. The devoted sculptor
faithfully paid tribute to the magnitude of
Ozymandias's might, but now that faithful
tribute remains in stone to serve as a
mockery. Obviously, Ozymandias is not alive
to be embarrassed by his boast that calls
attention to his now nonexistent kingdom
and faded glories. Nevertheless, his words
and image continue to taunt the waned splendor
of both colossal king and colossal statue.

These ruins of today were once a marvel of
the world, just as Ozymandias was once a
marvel among kings and expected to remain so.
The irony lies within the fact that neither
Ozymandias's memory nor his statue remain
completely intact, and Shelley seems
adequately to develop that theme by stressing
supporting ironies in setting, situation,
and thought.

Exercise

1. Construct an outline from this essay. Break the essay down into its parts and identify those parts.
2. Explain the student's apparent pattern of logical order. Why did she arrange the paragraphs as she did? Is this arrangement effective? Why or why not?
3. What key words are used to connect paragraphs to each other and to connect sentences within paragraphs to each other?
4. Mark sentences of discussion that *comment* on the evidence. How do these sentences relate to the thesis statement? Explain.

The procedure mapped out in this chapter has described the preparation of the most basic form of technical analysis: analyzing one literary feature to demonstrate its reflection of theme. More complex essays are of course possible. You could be asked to analyze more than one feature. You might be asked to compare the techniques of different authors or to compare the technique of the same author in two different works. And you could be asked to incorporate research into your essay—that is, to use professional critics to help you make your analysis.

Such complications would certainly force you to reconsider your focus. You might have to broaden your thesis or alter your plan of procedure. The length of your essay could increase, and the purpose of individual paragraphs could change. Still, if you truly understand the nature of analysis and the basic compositional technique for it, more sophisticated writing assignments should pose no really new writing problems.

STUDY QUESTIONS AND PAPER TOPICS FOR SPECIFIC TYPES OF ANALYSIS

As you select a topic for your paper, you would do well to review the categories of literary elements listed in your textbook. What follows here is a list of study questions for each category that should stimulate your thinking on the subject, guide you in annotating the text of the work of literature, and lead you to some determinations about what it is important for you to discuss in your essay.

Although the characteristics are grouped in your table of contents under the larger headings of "Fiction," "Poetry," and "Drama," there can be much overlapping; the same characteristics can appear in different forms of literature. For example, plot and characterization are discussed under fiction in your text. But a play or narrative poem uses plot and characterization in its development, so the same study question could apply in your preparation of a paper on poetry or drama. You could write a very worthwhile paper on the characterization of either the duke or his last wife in

Browning's "My Last Duchess," for instance. Be creative in developing your paper topics. Also included are hypothetical essay titles that might suggest paper topics to you.

Fiction

Plot

- Why are the events of the story arranged as they are?
- What is the primary conflict and how does it reflect theme?
- Where is the climax? What does it reveal about the purpose of the story?
- What happens after the climax? How does it comment on the significance of the climax?
- What are the segments of the plot structure? Why is the story divided in this way?
- What moves the story line along? External action? Internal conflicts within characters? Both?

- ESSAY TITLES:
    —The Anticlimactic Climax of *A Hunger Artist*
    —Old Badman Brown: Those Morning-After Blues
    —The Significance of External Action in *An Occurrence at Owl Creek Bridge*

Focus and Voice

- Who tells the story and what difference does this make?
- Is the point of view omniscient or dramatic? What difference does this make?
- Is the focus fixed or mobile? Why is it so?
- How are the reader's perceptions guided or controlled by this focus?
- How does this focus help a reader see theme?
- Whose voice do we hear in the narration?

- What attitudes are reflected in the voice? What connotations in the words? How do these help point to theme?
- ESSAY TITLES:
  —A Touch of Class: The Narrator in *Our Friend Judith*
  —Growing Up Female: A Look at Voice in *Boys and Girls*

Characterization

- Who is the main character?
- What is he like, and how do we learn what he is like?
- How do his actions and conflicts reflect theme?
- Does he learn anything important in the course of the story or not? How does that reflect theme?
- Why are the other characters there? How do they contribute to plot? to theme? to the conflict of the main character?
- Are the characters round? flat? stereotypes? Why would the author develop them so?
- How is the character presented? How does he dress? What is his occupation? What are his surroundings like?
- ESSAY TITLES:
  —Back in the Saddle Again: Motivation in *The Rocking-Horse Winner*
  —The Presentation of Mangan's Sister in James Joyce's *Araby*
  —The Narrator as Character in *The Celebrated Jumping Frog of Calaveras County*

Symbols

- What in the story is symbolic?
- How do you know that it is a symbol?
- What is its meaning?
- At what points in the plot does the symbol appear?
- How often does it appear?
- How would the story be different if the symbol were not there?
- Is the symbol an archetype?

- ESSAY TITLES:
  —Symbolism in *The Lottery:* An Analysis of the Description of the Lottery Box
  —Name Symbolism in *Young Goodman Brown*

Poetry

Speaker

- Who is the speaker in the poem? Is there more than one speaker? If so, what is their relationship to each other?
- What facts do you have about the speaker's situation?
- What is the speaker's tone of voice and attitude toward the subject matter?
- What does the speaker's tone suggest about his character and personality?
- How would the poem be different with another speaker?
- ESSAY TITLES:
  —His Lady's Response in "Dover Beach"
  —The Emotional State of the Speaker in "Stopping by Woods on a Snowy Evening": Two Interpretations
  —Tone in Dorothy Parker's "Comment"
  —The Evolving Attitude of the Speaker in "Fern Hill"

Situation and Setting

- What exactly is going on in the poem?
- Who is involved? Where? When? Why?
- What do you know about where things take place?
- What descriptive details are used to establish setting?
- What is significant about the descriptive detail? Is it suggestive? Of what?
- How would it affect the poem if the setting were different?
- ESSAY TITLES:
  —Setting as the Trigger of Poetic Impulse in "Among School Children"

—The Ritual of the Wake in "After Great Pain"
—First Impressions: A Study of Setting in the Opening of "The Love Song of J. Alfred Prufrock"

Words

- Is there ambiguity in any of the words? Do any have double meanings?
- What is the effect of the ambiguity on the meaning of the poem?
- Do any words have significant connotations?
- Are there patterns in the words? Do various words have similar connotations? Do various words seem selected to create the same impact?

- ESSAY TITLES:
  —The Harvest of Words: An Analysis of Language in "To Autumn"
  —Religious Connotations in "Spring and Fall"

Figurative Language

- How do metaphors and similes in the poem sharpen the images?
- Are there connotations suggested in these comparisons?
- If there is personification, why would the poet choose to use it? How does it affect or influence the reader's perception of the poem?
- If there is a symbol, what kind is it? A symbolic thing? action? event?
- How do you know it is a symbol? How is it used in the poem?
- What is its significance? How does it add meaning to the poem?

- ESSAY TITLES:
  —Metaphor in "The Brain Is Wider than the Sky"
  —Symbolism in "When Lilacs Last in the Dooryard Bloomed"

Sound and Sight

- Are there repetitions of sounds that form a significant pattern?
- What is the effect of the rhythm? Is it slow and mournful? quick and happy?
- How does the rhythm complement the poem's meaning?
- What is the effect of the sound of individual words or a series of words? Is the sound soft and melodic? Is it harsh and abrasive?
- What is the relationship between the sound of the words and the meaning of the poem?
- Are there any significant visual features in the poem?
- How do they affect the reader?
- How do they complement the poem's meaning?

- ESSAY TITLES:
  —Pacing in "The Second Coming"
  —Sound in "Kubla Khan": The Sacred River of Words

Stanza and Verse Form

- What is the stanza form of the poem? the verse form?
- Do they follow a traditional pattern or are they the inventions of the poet?
- How do these forms enhance the effect of the poetry?

- ESSAY TITLES:
  —Creative Verse Form in "Chanson Innocente"
  —Sonnet Form in Shakespeare's "Winter" and "Spring": A Study in Consistency

Drama

Dramatic Structure and the Stage

- What is the climax or peripety of the play?
- Where does the action break into the five structural parts: exposition, rising action, climax, falling action, catastrophe?

- For what kind of stage does the play seem intended? How would the staging affect the play's visual impact on the audience?

- ESSAY TITLES:
  —The Play behind the Play: A Rationale for the Off-Stage Action in *Hedda Gabler*
  —The Ritual of Plot in *The Sacrifice of Isaac*
  —Staging *The Sacrifice of Isaac*

Tragedy, Comedy, and the Modern Drama

- How are the values and principles of the characters derived in the play? Where do they come from? Are they universal, as in tragedy? societal, as in comedy? or more personal, as in modern drama?
- How are these values involved in the dilemma of the central character or characters?
- How many central characters are there? Is there a single tragic hero? a multitude of comic characters? a core of central modern characters? What difference does this make in the focus, purpose, and impact of the play?
- How does the play end? With tragic enlightenment? With comic conformity to social roles? Or with a more complex modern situation that must be analyzed on its own terms?

- ESSAY TITLES:
  —The Impossibility of Being Ernest: Jack Worthing as Comic Character
  —The Predictability of Ending in *Hamlet*

Evaluating
Literature

4

Why is it that some works of literature endure? What is it about a poem or story or play that touches many people in many generations? What makes a work of literature great?

Students of literature—not just those currently enrolled in college English courses, but people everywhere of all ages who love literature—never finish answering these questions. The greater your capacities for responding, the more moving a great work of literature will be for you. In turn, this response will help you to grow even more as a person, and the more you develop as a human being, the more you can understand what makes a work of literature great.

All along the way, nevertheless, you stop and pass judgment on what you read. This term you have probably asked a classmate, "How did you like that story we had for today?" You doubtless were ready with opinions of your own. You may have sometimes found your opinions in conflict with your instructor's, and you may have wondered why a play like *Hamlet* seems to be everywhere you turn.

There is no ready answer as to what exactly makes a work of literature great. In searching for pat answers some students do themselves great harm by making false, easy assumptions about what determines greatness in a work, creating myths we might just as well dispense with now. These "myths" are by no means entirely false; it is, in fact, the element of truth in them that makes them so easy to believe.

MYTHS ABOUT WHAT MAKES A WORK OF LITERATURE GREAT

1. *"Important" subject.* Some people make the mistake of assuming greatness in a work of literature if it deals with an important subject. But a story about one man laying down his life for another can be poorly told, overly sentimental, and have shallow characterization and clichéd situations. On the other hand, look at John Stone's "Coming Home," a poem about riding home as a child in the back seat of the car. How "important" is the subject? This question cannot be answered simply. The greatness of a work of literature depends on what the author does with the subject matter.

2. *Serious tone.* Some people confuse a serious tone, brooding characters, and sad ending with greatness. While many great works of literature have these characteristics, others certainly do not. The greatness of a work will be reflected in how the tone contributes to the overall effectiveness of the story, but there are no simple formulas for making judgments. None of the major characters in *The Importance of Being Earnest* is serious, and much of what

they say is downright silly. But this fine play is nevertheless a serious satire on the manners and morals of England's idle rich.

3. *Obscure language and images.* If you cannot understand it, it must be great, right? Wrong. Many great works of literature do offer ideas and portray feelings not fully or easily understood in one reading, but if a good reader cannot find meaning in some cryptic lines of a particular poem, he would be a fool to call the poem "great." Obscurity does not equal greatness.

4. *A shining moral.* A work of literature is not great simply because a character or the narrator or speaker states some great moral truth within its lines or pages. Any responsible judgment of greatness involves an assessment of that statement in the context of the whole work of literature, along with assessments of many elements of the work and how they *all* work together. No single thing can make a work of literature great.

5. *A "great" author.* Authors have their highs and lows. The belief that anything by Yeats has got to be good, for example, is faulty. It may be logical to look and hope for greatness in the work of a proven author; there are, however, no assurances that you will find it.

Exercise

The movie, theatre, and book reviews you read in the newspaper are one type of essay of critical judgment. Observing how professional reviewers approach assignments may help you to write your essay. Prepare the exercises below.

1. Select from a newspaper or magazine the review of a movie, play, or book with which you are familiar. Explain why you agree or disagree with the review. Comment on specific points the writer makes about particular features of the work. What other points would you have raised if you had written the review?

2. Find two reviews of a movie that you have seen in which the reviewers disagree about the quality of the

movie. What review is better? Why? Do you agree with the judgment rendered in that review?

RECOGNIZING GREATNESS IN A WORK OF LITERATURE

Recognizing greatness in a work of literature comes only with an earnest study of literature in general. Reading and studying the works of literature that textbooks and instructors hold up to you as great will help you to set high standards. But often these works of literature are poems, short stories, and plays for which you need to develop a taste. What is so good about them may not be readily apparent to you. Whoever liked his first olive? Your appreciation of literature must be carefully nurtured to help you to develop your responses and to understand them. Most people unfamiliar with ballet see the "greatness" in a dancer when he bounds and leaps across the stage. Anyone who dances seriously or knows ballet well understands that while the leaps are exciting, it is the smaller foot movements that are difficult to master and that are the true test of a dancer's mettle. As you study literature and read with your teacher, your understanding of greatness continues to develop. You come to learn that *the greatness of a work of literature depends entirely upon the treatment of the subject matter and upon the work's richness, depth, and complexity.* What does the author do with his material? How moving or effective is the treatment? Aristotle explains that the greatness of a dramatic tragedy is intimately tied to its ability to cause a catharsis in the audience. Such greatness is accomplished by a genius that causes all of the elements you have studied separately, such as plot, theme, symbolism, and imagery, to come together to move an audience and to create something greater than simply the sum of its various parts.

As you set yourself to the task of evaluating a work of literature and writing about this evaluation, start with your personal response. Does the work of literature involve you, move you?

Exercise

Works of literature are grouped together below because they have similar themes or deal with the same type of subject matter. Discuss the differences in the ways these themes and subjects are treated in the different works. How do the apparent intentions of the authors differ? In what different ways are the works developed? Which work in each group would you say is the greater one (not that literature is a contest)? Why? Is it too close to call? Why?

1. "My Last Duchess" and "I sat next to the duchess at tea" (limerick)
2. "The Rose Family" and "One Perfect Rose"
3. "The Turtle" and "The Flea"
4. *Her First Ball* and *Araby*

WRITING THE ESSAY OF CRITICAL JUDGMENT

Francis Bacon said:

> Reading maketh a full man,
> conference [conversation] a
> ready man, and writing an exact man.

Writing an essay of critical judgment can often be the incentive you need to sit down and decide how you really judge a work of literature. With this type of essay, perhaps more than with most others, you will find your ideas evolving while you try to compose your thoughts. The more you play with the ideas and try to figure out what you want to say in your paper, the more value you will discover in a truly great work of literature (and the more dissatisfied you will feel with a second-rate work). You may find yourself responding more as you try to pinpoint what makes it all come together to work so well. There are, of course, ranges of quality—from awful to fair to good to great. Never will there be universal agreement on the quality of any single work, so the best you can do is to back your judgment up with a substantive discussion of specific features of the poem or story or play.

In trying to arrive at your determination of value and to explain it in an essay, you may find it useful to compare the process to that of collecting scraps of tinfoil and shaping them into a ball, as you may have done as a child, gathering the shiny bits wherever you found them and watching with satisfaction as the ball grew and grew. When you write your essay, the first bit of foil you pick up will be whatever struck you most about the work of literature. Maybe it was a character you liked, a relationship between two characters, a description of the setting, the language, a striking image, or the theme.

After you decide what is so good about this feature and explain it to yourself in notes or a first draft or an outline, see where this discussion leads you. For instance, if you start with a main character who you thought was so enthralling that you found you really cared *what happened to him*, then consider discussing the quality of *the plot*. Did the author do a good job of developing what happened to this character? Keep adding on bits of foil as you consider different features of the work and then look at the size of the figurative sphere you have created. Is it massive, as the one for *Hamlet* would be? Is it shiny but small, as for a well executed limerick. Or is it somewhere in between, suggesting a solid work of literature, but one you would nevertheless hesitate to call great.

Be honest with yourself and with your reader as you state your general assessment. Few works of literature are all good or all bad; they have their strong points and their weak points. Some features, you will decide, do not shine enough to be a part of the tinfoil sphere.

Let your reactions to the work be your guide. As you were reading, what did you find pleasurable or disturbing? Was there one character you were glad to see each time he entered the story? Were there long, descriptive passages you found tedious? Begin with these reactions, analyze them, determine how legitimate they are, and select your material from those that seem best founded. If you work in this way, you will probably discover that you have more material than you can fit into your essay. You will discover also that some of your initial responses were valid while others were not. Concentrate on the sound ones. Some will be easier for you to develop in your essay than will others. Some will illustrate the basic point of your essay more emphatically than will others. When it comes time to commit words to paper, you will discover where your best examples lie. But begin with your genuine responses because a more mechanical approach is likely to lead to a stilted paper that sounds insincere. And you must take all these matters into account before you render a final judgment.

You are likely to find that time and space will not allow you to discuss every characteristic you have reviewed in coming to your evaluation. If you are limited, for example, to a five-page paper due in three days, you must select for discussion those features that will best illustrate your main point. While the greatness of the work certainly depends on all these qualities being effectively integrated, your essay will have to focus on the best examples.

Exercise

Comment on the strong and weak points in each of these works. Which characteristics move them toward greatness? What qualities keep them from being perfect? Which of the poems would you say is the greatest? Why? Which is the furthest from greatness? Why? Which of the stories is the greatest? Which of the plays?

1. "When Lilacs Last in the Dooryard Bloomed"
2. "Uneasy Rider"
3. "Cherrylog Road"
4. "Marks"
5. "The Word *Plum*"

1. *The Cask of Amontillado*
2. *Beyond the Bayou*
3. *Araby*

1. *The Sacrifice of Isaac*
2. *Hedda Gabler*

ORGANIZING AND DEVELOPING THE DRAFT

The organization of this paper's outline should follow the standard form prescribed throughout this book. Below is a paragraph by paragraph description of the basic organization of the essay of critical judgment. ·

PARAGRAPH 1:
- opening
- thesis statement indicating your basic critical evaluation of the work of literature
- statement of procedure, perhaps indicating that you will discuss the quality of certain characteristics of the work

PARAGRAPH 2:
- you may wish to place a one-paragraph summary of the work here to acquaint the reader with the ideas that you are going to discuss and to make subsequent reference to characters and situations easier and smoother

PARAGRAPH 3 (first paragraph of working body of essay):
- topic sentence: introduce evaluation of the first characteristic as part of the overall evaluation stated in the thesis
- detail sentences: develop evidence and commentary to persuade your audience

PARAGRAPH 4:
- topic sentence: introduce evaluation of the next literary characteristic to support the thesis
- detail sentences: develop evidence and commentary to persuade your reader

PARAGRAPH 5:
- same as paragraph 4, but discussing yet another characteristic

CONCLUSION:
- In addition to reasserting your thesis and striking a note of finality, the conclusion in an argumentative essay can have an additional purpose: anti-thesis. In other words, if your evaluation of the work has been basically positive, is there any glaring negative feature you think it is wise and fair to mention here? *Do not end on this note of anti-*

thesis. Mention it in the conclusion, then reassert your thesis and strike the note of finality.

Review this sample essay.

The Glass Menagerie: Good, Solid Drama

 Tennessee Williams's The Glass Menagerie is the sad story of a fragile family. It is a moving play that involves the audience in the lives of the Wingfield family on an evening when Amanda, the mother, and Tom and Laura, her grown children, finally have to face realities about themselves. The play is well done with clever symbolism and strong character development underscoring a universal theme. The pain of the people in the play as they face realities they can no longer escape draws on the sympathies of the audience.

 On this particular evening in the life of the Wingfields, a "gentleman caller" is coming to visit Laura. At the nagging insistence of his mother, Tom has invited a friend from work for dinner. Trying to act nonchalantly about this major event Amanda says simply, "I remember suggesting that it would be nice for your sister if you brought home some nice young man from the warehouse. I think that I've made that suggestion more than once." As they prepare for this great event, we learn about them as individuals and as a family. We learn of Laura's insecurities and shyness about her crippled leg. We learn about Amanda's desperation over her daughter's lack of social success and her longing for old times when she was supposedly the belle of the ball. And we learn about the strain of family responsibility on Tom, whose father long ago deserted, and his need for escape and freedom. When it turns out that Jim-- the gentleman caller--has a fiancée, all the Wingfields must face reality. For Tom

and Laura, it's a turning point. For their
mother, it is a final crushing blow.

All of the themes in this play, which can
generally be put under the heading of
"facing reality," are important ones that
most people can identify with. We all suffer
one or more of the problems of the members
of the Wingfield family and try to escape
them as they do. Most of us have had some
form of Laura's insecurities, especially as
teenagers when it is so hard to accept
imperfections in ourselves. The older we get,
the more we find ourselves burdened with
responsibilities like Tom's, which often
seem to smother us as he felt smothered.
"Man is by instinct a lover, a hunter, a
fighter, and none of those instincts are
given much play at the warehouse." When
things get too bad, it's easy to drift in
Amanda's kind of golden memories embroidered
to be more beautiful than the past ever
really was. We see her escape into bygone
times when she explains to Laura, "This is
the dress in which I led the cotillion.
Won the cakewalk twice at Sunset Hill, wore
one Spring to the Governor's Ball in Jackson."
The themes in this play are about everyday
experiences that mean a great deal to people.
It is about how people live their lives and
see themselves.

The ideas in this play are important because they touch a nerve in many of us who
are struggling to cope with similar problems.
Most of us have things in our lives that have
not turned out the way we had hoped. Like
the characters in the play, we also build
up defense mechanisms, a way to cope. Laura
has her glass animals; Amanda has her memories;
and Tom goes to the movies.

Laura's escape to her glass menagerie brings
us to one of the best technical features of
the play, symbolism. Laura's glass animal
figurines are too fragile to move from the

shelf. She warns Jim, the gentleman caller,
about how fragile they are.

> Most of them are little animals made
> out of glass, the tiniest little animals
> in the world. . . . Here's an example
> of one, if you'd like to see it. . . . Oh,
> be careful--if you breathe, it breaks!

They are like the fragile Wingfields, also on
the shelf, too afraid, for various reasons,
to try to live life. They seem to be afraid
that they might break just like the glass
animals. One of the animals, the unicorn,
seems to represent Laura. Its horn makes it
an oddity among horses the way Laura's leg
separates her from other girls. The parallel
is seen when Laura knocks the unicorn off
the shelf while she is dancing with Jim. She
is not upset, but points out that "maybe it's
a blessing in disguise. . . . I'll just
imagine he had an operation. The horn was
removed to make him feel less--freakish."
For a moment Laura became like other girls,
happy and dancing. She and the unicorn lost
what made them different. Jim's visit
changed both of them for good. Williams's
excellent use of symbolism helps us to
appreciate what is happening to Laura.
 Another feature of the play, character
development, is also superior. Tennessee
Williams takes Amanda, for example, and
makes her come alive with her dialogue, her
frustrations and motivations, and the way
she treats her children. Her language is
often that of the Southern Belle. She
reflects a refinement her life no longer has.
She no longer has "seventeen gentlemen
callers" or even one husband! Her daughter
is not a belle, and her son is a reminder
of his father. We see all these complex
parts of her psychology in everything she
says. We see it when she advises Laura that

"all pretty girls are a trap, a pretty
trap, and men expect them to be." We hear
it again when she flirts with Jim.

> Well, well, well, so this is
> Mr. O'Connor. Introductions
> entirely unnecessary. I've
> heard so much about you
> from my boy. I finally said
> to him, Tom--good gracious!--
> why don't you bring this
> paragon to supper?

And we are struck by her tone when she
lashes out at Tom.

> That's right, now that
> you've had us make such fools
> of ourselves. The effort,
> the preparations, all the ex-
> pense! The new floor lamp, the
> rug, the clothes for Laura!
> All for what? To entertain
> some other girl's fiancé! Go
> to the movies, go!

She is a tortured woman whose wants are
excellently developed by a powerful playwright.

Although this is a strong play that is in
most ways successful, there was one disturbing feature. Throughout the play, "images"
and "legends" are flashed on a screen behind
the characters to comment on the action that
is going on. For example, when Amanda is
about to open the door for Jim after a
frightened Laura has refused to, the word
"Terror" is flashed on the screen. This seems
disruptive and distracts the audience attention, keeping them from getting involved in
the play itself. Perhaps The Glass Menagerie
would be better without this gimmick. In
most every other way, it is a beautiful play
well worth reading or seeing.

Exercise

1. Observe and mark all words in the essay that indicate judgment or evaluation by the student writer.
2. What key words are repeated in the thesis and topic sentences?
3. Comment on the student's use of quotations. Are there enough? Too many? Are they effective?
4. Why are the body paragraphs arranged as they are? How do you know?
5. How does the essay's conclusion reflect the student's thesis?

A FINAL WORD ON THE MATTER: PERSONAL OPINIONS VS. CRITICAL OPINIONS

You probably believe that in literature as in most other things you know what you like. You have certainly enjoyed some of the works you have read for your course more than others. Maybe you generally enjoy a love story more than an adventure story or a comedy more than a tragedy. Tastes differ from person to person, but one person's taste differs too, over time. As a student, you would do well to keep your mind open to the new experiences of literature that you encounter in the classroom. Works that seem strange or difficult at first, you may soon learn to like. In any case, it is important for you to understand the difference between your personal opinion (*taste*) and your critical opinion (*judgment*).

It is often said that there is no accounting for tastes, and so it is foolish to argue whether chocolate ice cream is better than raspberry sherbet. Either you like it better or you don't. You can, however, discriminate between brands of ice cream, critically judging the merits of one over the other, noting ingredients, flavor, and texture. Both types of opinions are valuable and important. The more you *study* literature, the more your personal and critical opinions may begin to overlap as you develop a taste for things you may not have enjoyed before.

Exercise

Read each of the following statements. Which reflect purely personal opinions of taste? Which are critical opinions of judgment? Explain your answers.

1. I love science fiction stories.
2. A story with animals in it cannot be all bad.
3. The plot was pretty believable.
4. The movie was just beautiful to look at.
5. I liked the main character. I thought he was very convincing.
6. The idea was interesting, but I just hate poetry.
7. It is really exciting, if you like detective stories.
8. The play had a good message, but there was some really bad acting.
9. I like that actor, but he was all wrong for the part.

Writing about Literature in Other Ways

5

The papers discussed in the last three chapters—summaries and explications, analyses, and critical judgments—are the most familiar and basic types of literary essays. To some degree, all your assignments will develop into one or more of these types. But there are special assignments that only partly fit into one of these categories. This chapter will discuss briefly other typical paper assignments made in literature classes: imitations and parodies; reactions and replies; essays defining critical terms; analyses of contexts (literary, historical, political, religious, etc.); comparison and contrast essays; and essay examinations.

IMITATIONS

Writing imitations of an author's work can be both a wonderful amusement and a serious lesson in literature. Imitations are sincere efforts at copying the style and content of an author's work. The purpose of imitation is not necessarily either to praise or to ridicule the author and his work, although some imitations mock or poke fun at an author. Imitation intends to recreate the flavor of the original.

The purpose of having you write imitations in the college classroom is to cause you, in yet another way, to analyze and to appreciate what a writer says and how he says it. Writing a good imitation can also bring a great deal of personal satisfaction to a student who discovers a talent for creative writing.

If you are going to paint an imitation of a Botticelli painting, you first have to survey his subject matter—to discover what kinds of things appear in his work. When you realize that plowhorses or circus scenes are inappropriate, you perhaps choose a Roman goddess, knowing about his *Venus* and *Three Graces*. Once you have your subject matter, you look for elements of technique. What types of colors did he routinely use? What kind of brush strokes? What kind of line? lighting? And so on.

If you were writing an imitation of Hemingway, you might put a central male character in a life-threatening situation of high adventure. Your language would be bold, simple, and direct. To imitate any author, you must recognize qualities characteristic of his or her writing.

Exercise

1. What suggestions would you make for imitations of the work of these artists?
   Richard Wagner
   e. e. cummings
   Samuel Clemens
   Dorothy Parker

Fred Astaire
Elvis Presley
Grandma Moses

Notice that the more distinctive the artist's work, the easier it is to imitate. List characteristics of the work of each artist that are obvious examples of features to imitate.

2. Practice imitations of the works of the authors listed below. When you finish explain: (a) how you chose your subject matter, and (b) what points of style or manner you were consciously trying to imitate.

E. A. Robinson
e. e. cummings
Edgar Allan Poe

PARODIES

An interesting twist on imitations is to use the style of one author with the content of another or vice versa. Do they fit comfortably, or do they chafe and begin to suggest parody?

Parody in general is a type of imitation that intends to comment on the original author's work or on the author himself. The parodist usually pokes fun through an imitation of one piece of work in which the manner or the matter (or both) of the original work has been exaggerated for effect, much like caricatures in political cartoons and impressions of famous people by nightclub comedians.

Read from *Hamlet,* act 5, scene 1, lines 156–65, and then read Frost's "Stopping by Woods on a Snowy Evening." When you have finished, read and discuss the poem below.

Whose skull this is I think I know.
His body's in the churchyard though.
He will not see me stopping here
To pick his bones, Horatio!

Alas, poor Yorick. It seems queer
Who rode me piggyback far and near
Around the woods by Elsinore Lake
Doth now ride maggots in his ear.

I'll give your little head a shake
To see if there's been some mistake.
Where fled your smiles, beloved Creep?
Your lip is now but downy flake.

Your skull is lovely, dark, and deep.
But I have promises to keep
And kin to kill before I sleep.
And kin to kill before I sleep.

What is the effect of putting Shakespeare's content into Frost's style? What is the effect of changing the rhythm and meter of the original speech? Does the stanza form adopted from Frost provide a legitimate organization of the speech? How is the tone different from the original? What effect does this change have on an audience?

Review the poem line by line to point out and explain specific similarities to the Frost poem that tie the two together and create the effect of parody.

Exercise

Practice blending the styles of these authors.

1. Rewrite "To the Virgins, to Make Much of Time" in the style of "Harlem."
2. Rewrite a portion of "The Love Song of J. Alfred Prufrock" in the style of "Frankie and Johnnie."
3. Rewrite the opening of *The Short Happy Life of Francis Macomber* in the style of *The Zebra Storyteller*.

You approach writing parody as you would imitation, except that you have an ulterior motive—to poke fun at the content and/or style of the author. Look for characteristics to exaggerate (Hemingway's sentence structure, cummings's typographical tricks, Pinter's choppy dialogue). Perhaps you may decide to develop a serious imitation of style as you ridicule content. Think of the mimic who, sounding like some stern and serious presidential candidate, opens his mouth as if to deliver a campaign speech only to sing something ridiculous like "I Feel Pretty." Or imagine how ludicrous a recipe for turkey stuffing would sound in the language of Shakespeare.

Perhaps you might imitate the content of the original seriously while embellishing the style for parody. Those who mimic Ted Kennedy get laughs by saying nothing more than "Good evening, ladies and gentlemen," as long as they exaggerate his Boston accent. A scene from Hamlet rewritten in the style of modern slang with no restraint or understatement on Hamlet's part might create a humorous opportunity for that poor young man to get things off his chest. If you're really ambitious, you might exaggerate both content and style.

Exercise

An easy way to begin working with parody is to concoct satirical subtitles for actual works.

As a class, develop several alternate titles for each of these works. Explain your motives.

Examples: "Dover Beach: Soliloquy of a Manic-Depressive"

"Mr. Flood's Party" or "The Tilbury Senior Citizens Program"

The Lottery or *I Remember Mama*

1. *A Hunger Artist*
2. *The Rocking-Horse Winner*
3. "Aunt Jennifer's Tigers"
4. "The Ruined Maid"
5. *The Glass Menagerie*

Exercise

Discuss as a class plans of attack for a parody of something you have recently read and discussed. When you have written your parodies, compare and contrast them. What did you learn about the original work that you had not noticed before your efforts at parody?

REACTIONS AND REPLIES

Sometime you may be asked to write a paper for which you are not given a specific purpose or form. Your teacher hopes that *you* will discover a purpose for your paper by developing a topic *you* consider worthwhile rather than one you have been told is worthwhile. Your teacher might also hope that if you are committed to the paper topic, you will automatically develop an appropriate essay form or will at least be willing to search for one.

In such assignments you are asked to react or reply to the literature. Your instructor might ask you to keep a journal in which you write whatever thoughts arise as you read a work. Your instructor might ask you to develop these reactions into a full-length essay. Or your instructor might even ask you to talk back to the author about whatever it is you think he should hear from one of his readers.

All of these writing assignments and others of the free-form variety will involve personal and critical judgments. Remember from Chapter 4 the distinction between personal opinions of taste and critical opinions of judgment. While personal opinions are valid, they are different in character from critical opinions.

In papers of reaction and reply, you are encouraged to express personal opinions and to explore their significance. These papers give you the chance to talk about the satisfaction you are or are not getting from your reading.

Keep the following questions in mind as you read for a reaction paper:

1. Do you like the characters or not? Why?
2. Do any of the characters remind you of a public figure or someone you know personally? How does this similarity affect your response?
3. Is the situation in the story similar to a situation in which you have found yourself? How does this similarity influence your response?
4. How does the language of the work of literature strike you? Was it easy or difficult for you to follow?

5. Was there something you particularly liked or disliked about the work? Explore the reasons behind this reaction.
6. Did this piece of literature remind you of any other work you have studied? Was it similar or different? How does the comparison affect your response?
7. Did the work of literature remind you of anything you have been studying in another course? Did one course of study shed any light on the other?

Work through these exercises, which will help you to focus on your responses to the literature in order to turn them into worthwhile essays.

Exercise

Write a one- or two-sentence response to these titles. What goes through your mind as you read them? If you have already read the works, try to imagine you are seeing the titles for the first time and do not know what the literature is about, beyond what the title suggests.
1. *The Artificial Nigger*
2. *A Very Old Man with Enormous Wings*
3. "Uneasy Rider"
4. "Barbie Doll"
5. "My Lady's Presence Makes the Roses Red"
6. *The Importance of Being Earnest*
7. *The Dumb Waiter*

Exercise

Read the following poem and write a response to each of the ideas underlined. What occurs to you as you read them. Look for a pattern in your answers.

Coming Home

About two thousand miles
   into my life
the family bounced south
   <u>west   east</u>   1
<u>in an old Oldsmobile.</u>   2

<u>Two brothers tumbled</u>   3
   on the back seat

watching the world blur
upside down right side up
  through windows
  timed fogged in
slowly from the corners.

   Nights
cars came at us
  wall-eyed
their lights sliding
  over the ceiling
like <u>night fighters</u>   4

  while in the front
<u>they talked parental low</u>   5
  in a drone
  we didn't hear
tossing through Arkansas
  toward Mississippi.

When our eyes grew red
  and blood bulged
in our heads from laughing
  <u>we slept</u>   6
<u>he on the seat</u>
  <u>and I bent over</u>
<u>the humped transmission</u>   6

<u>close to the only motor</u>
  <u>in the world.</u>   > 7

1.
2.
3.
4.
5.
6.
7.
8.

- Did you take long car trips as a child?
- Do you have a brother?

- Are you a brother?
- Or are you a mother, father, or sister? What is your experience in a similar situation?
- Does the poem seem familiar or exotic to you?

Consider the differences between members of your class and how these differences might make for a range of responses to this poem. Consider the age, sex, and the ethnic, cultural, and economic backgrounds of the members of the group. You may learn more about the poem thanks to the insight of someone whose experience is different from your own.

ESSAYS THAT DEFINE A CRITICAL TERM

The study of literature is filled with critical terms that classify types of literature. These terms include, for example, tragedy, romanticism, satire, sonnet, naturalism, and all the technical characteristics discussed in Chapter 3. These terms help the literary critic to identify and classify phenomena at work in the literature. It is helpful to recognize these phenomena as members of a class because often in literature one example may illuminate another.

Because some of these terms may be new to you, your instructor might wish to reinforce their meaning for you by asking you to write an essay that defines a term by explaining how it works in a sample of the literature. This assignment is the one that Aristotle gave to himself when he wrote the *Poetics*. In the *Poetics* Aristotle defines and explains what tragedy is by showing how it works in Sophocles' play *Oedipus Tyrannus*, which appears in your text.

Your basic question in such an essay is: *How* is this work an example of *this type*.

Exercise

Explain briefly how each of the following works might be used to explain, through example, the classification printed next to the title:

LITERARY EXAMPLE	TYPE
1. *The Importance of Being Earnest*	comedy
2. *Hamlet*	tragedy
3. *The Short Happy Life of Francis Macomber*	realism
4. Young Goodman Brown (the character)	protagonist
5. "Aunt Jennifer's Tigers"	symbolism
6. "The Death of the Ball Turret Gunner"	metaphor
7. "There once was a spinster of Ealing"	limerick
8. "Dirge"	free verse
9. *An Occurrence at Owl Creek Bridge*	psychological realism
10. "Ozymandias"	irony

The best way to explain an idea is by way of a good example. Your reader (and you too) might develop a greater understanding and appreciation of free verse through reading your explanation of how it operates in a poem like "Dirge" and why it is used.

A paper in which you define a critical term by example enhances your appreciation of both the category or literary type and the specific poem, play, or story you use to explain it.

ANALYSES OF CONTEXTS

In introductory literature classes, poems, short stories, and plays are often talked about in isolation. They are discussed as pure art forms. In literary survey courses and other advanced English classes, works are frequently discussed in their social and historical frameworks.

In such courses, the purpose of studying literature is not just to study the art form but to study also how literature both reflects and influences what is going on in the world. From a work of literature we may learn about the history, politics, religion, philosophy, art, entertainment, customs, and mores of society.

It may be your purpose in a literary essay to connect a work to the society in which it was written. You may be asked to place the work in context, to set it in a framework.

As you do, remember to go beyond subject matter. It is easy enough to say that a certain poem deals with the violence in modern society. But look deeper. Do verse form, word choice, sound, and characterization also place it in that context of violence? Is its style as well as its message reflective of the time in which it was written?

Exercise

Comment on how thought and idea in these works are tied to the historical context:
1. "The Death of the Ball Turret Gunner"
2. "London, 1802"
3. *Young Goodman Brown*
4. "One Perfect Rose"
5. "On the Late Massacre in Piedmont"
Name five works of literature that are not so clearly tied to an historical era. Explain your choices.
1.
2.
3.
4.
5.

Exercise

Explain how style and technique in each of the following reflect the work's historical context. What is it about technique in each of these works that is typical of literature of the day?
1. *Her First Ball*
2. "A Valediction: Forbidding Mourning"
3. "You Too? Me Too—Why Not? Soda Pop"

4. 1)a
5. The Twenty-Third Psalm
6. *Hamlet*

Another context you might be asked to analyze is the relationship of authors and their works to each other. You might be asked, for example, to analyze the work of writers of the "Lost Generation" to see how both Fitzgerald and Hemingway, though their work is quite different, nevertheless portray the same malaise, one that affected many of their contemporaries.

There are also many long-standing literary traditions that produce works ripe for such analyses. War poems, love poems, and poems written to commemorate public events have been written for centuries. Comparing several works from different times can make for a fruitful study.

Exercise

Identify other literary traditions represented by works listed in your table of contents. Are there, for example, several religious poems that might be studied together?

ESSAYS OF COMPARISON AND CONTRAST

Comparison and contrast essays have always been a way for writers to discover new insights by looking at two or more things in the light of one another. We are able to understand, appreciate, and judge more thoroughly, confidently, and reasonably if we have a standard of comparison: "I never knew what hot was until I sat in my car in city traffic for two hours in mid-August." This statement shows insights into two situations: the hot time in August and all those times before when the speaker felt hot. The situations are comparable—both deal with the heat. But the point of the statements is contrast—the experiences were different. Just as comparison and contrast may show the difference between two similar things (hot weather then and now), they might also serve the purpose of showing similarities between two apparently different things: "Life is like a roller coaster; it has its ups and its downs."

In your literature class, you could run into quite a variety of kinds of comparison and contrast assignments. For example, you might be asked to compare the work of one author with that of another author who is (1) from the same or another historical period, (2) strikingly similar or different in his use of themes and techniques, or (3) reflective of a similar or a different social situation. For instance, how do Countee Cullen and Langston Hughes express the black experience differently? similarly?

Another type of comparison and contrast study you might be asked to make is one in which you look at two or more works of literature because they demonstrate (1) similar or different techniques, (2) similar or different themes, and (3) similar or different philosophical approaches to the same topic. Both Dylan Thomas in "Do Not Go Gentle into That Good Night" and Emily Dickinson in "Because I Could Not Stop for Death" treat the theme of dying. But the language, images, and tone of each reflect different attitudes. While Thomas calls for his father to "rage, rage against the dying of the light," Dickinson's persona gaily says of Death, "He kindly stopped for me."

Lastly, at other times you may be asked to compare and contrast one of an author's works with another of his or her works. Are the themes and techniques consistent? Do you find persistent patterns? Is the author's work different at different stages of his life? How is it different? Why might it be different? How do the various poems by Yeats in your text illuminate each other? What images and themes recur? What part do myths and the exotic play in his poetry?

Exercise

Explain why these authors might be coupled for comparison and contrast. (There may be many right answers.)

1. e. e. cummings and George Herbert

2. Shakespeare and Sophocles
3. John Donne and Gerard Manley Hopkins

List four pairs of authors that would make for good comparison and contrast analyses. Explain your selections.

1.
2.
3.
4.

Exercise

What possibilities for comparison and contrast analyses do you see with these couplings of literary works?

1. "Do Not Go Gentle into That Good Night"
   "Because I Could Not Stop for Death"
2. "The Passionate Shepherd to His Love"
   "To His Coy Mistress"
3. "The Word *Plum*"
   "Sound and Sense"
4. *The Short Happy Life of Francis Macomber*
   The Country Husband
5. *The Lottery*
   The Rocking-Horse Winner

Couple two works of literature for comparison and contrast: What similarities and differences are noteworthy?

Exercise

Compare and contrast these works by the same author.

1. E. A. Robinson: "Mr. Flood's Party" and "Richard Cory"
2. John Keats: "Ode to a Nightingale" and "Ode on a Grecian Urn"
3. William Blake: "London" and "The Tiger"
4. Emily Dickinson: "Wild Nights! Wild Nights!" and "A Narrow Fellow in the Grass"
5. John Donne: "A Valediction: Forbidding Mourning" and "Batter My Heart"

WRITING ESSAY EXAMINATIONS

Writing essay examinations is a fine art in itself. Understanding how to approach the composition of your essay answers can greatly improve your performance. Sometimes an intelligent student who has studied the material fails to do well on an essay exam because he or she does not handle this particular type of writing assignment effectively and correctly. This need not happen to you if you understand what an essay examination is for and how it really works. The thoughtful, conscientious student can learn to handle essay exams with skill.

Why Essay Examinations at All?

Why do instructors ask you to write essay examinations? Why won't short answer questions serve the purpose as well?

An objective test tries to discover what you don't know. An essay test tries to discover what you do know. Moreover, an essay examination creates the opportunity for yet another learning experience. A good essay exam need not simply test what you already know. It can also lead you to new awarenesses and a fuller understanding of concepts and principles you have been studying in class. Your instructor may not have an "answer" in mind and would like to learn from your essay. Writers learn more about their topics as they develop their thoughts into full sentences and paragraphs. Keeping the right attitude and leaving your mind open to new learning as you take your examination will give you a greater sense of freedom in developing a worthwhile response to a question.

Exercise

Give additional reasons that an instructor might wish you to take an essay examination. Discuss these with other members of your class and with your instructor.

Preparing for the Examination

Preparing for the examination includes everything that you do to get yourself ready to take the test, everything you do before you write your answer. It begins with your method of study. Of course you must read and understand the literature, and you must have listened to class lectures and discussion: There is no substitute for study and preparation.

But as you review the material, remember your purpose and the situation, and anticipate questions by keeping these pointers in mind.

1. What has been the slant of your course? Have you discussed the literature purely artistically? historically? politically?
2. What ideas or themes have been recurrent in the instructor's teaching of the material? Has your instructor frequently called your attention to verse forms or to how the literature shows various views of man's relation to society, for example? What words, phrases, or ideas recur frequently in your notes?
3. What patterns can you see in the types of authors selected or the types of readings assigned?

Exercise

Construct essay questions you might anticipate for a final examination in this course. Discuss them with your instructor.

1.

2.

3.

Acquaint yourself with significant passages from the works of literature. There's no need to memorize huge sections of the text, but your essay will seem and, in fact, will be more informed and authoritative if you include key words and phrases from the work(s) of literature you are discussing.

Exercise

What phrases from the following selections might be good to keep in mind for quoting in an essay examination?

The thousand injuries of Fortunato I had borne as I best could, but when he ventured upon insult I vowed revenge. You, who so well know the nature of my soul, will not suppose, however, that I gave utterance to a threat. *At length* I would be avenged; this was a point definitely settled—but the very definitiveness with which it was resolved precluded the idea of risk. I must not only punish but punish with impunity. A wrong is unredressed when retribution overtakes its redresser. It is equally unredressed when the avenger fails to make himself felt as such to him who has done the wrong.

It must be understood that neither by word nor deed had I given Fortunato cause to doubt my good will. I continued, as was my wont, to smile in his face, and he did not perceive that my smile *now* was at the thought of his immolation.

MY LAST DUCHESS

Ferrara

That's my last Duchess painted on the wall,
Looking as if she were alive. I call
That piece a wonder, now: Frà Pandolf's hands
Worked busily a day, and there she stands.
Will't please you sit and look at her? I said
"Frà Pandolf" by design, for never read
Strangers like you that pictured countenance,
The depth and passion of its earnest glance,
But to myself they turned (since none puts by
The curtain I have drawn for you, but I)
And seemed as they would ask me, if they durst,
How such a glance came there; so, not the first
Are you to turn and ask thus. Sir, 'twas not
Her husband's presence only, called that spot
Of joy into the Duchess' cheek: perhaps
Frà Pandolf chanced to say "Her mantle laps
Over my lady's wrist too much," or "Paint
Must never hope to reproduce the faint

Half-flush that dies along her throat": such stuff
Was courtesy, she thought, and cause enough
For calling up that spot of joy. She had
A heart—how shall I say?—too soon made glad,
Too easily impressed; she liked whate'er
She looked on, and her looks went everywhere.
Sir, 'twas all one! My favor at her breast,
The dropping of the daylight in the West,
The bough of cherries some officious fool
Broke in the orchard for her, the white mule
She rode with round the terrace—all and each
Would draw from her alike the approving speech,
Or blush, at least. She thanked men,—good! but thanked
Somehow—I know not how—as if she ranked
My gift of a nine-hundred-years-old name
With anybody's gift. Who'd stoop to blame
This sort of trifling? Even had you skill
In speech—which I have not—to make your will
Quite clear to such an one, and say, "Just this
Or that in you disgusts me; here you miss,
Or there exceed the mark"—and if she let
Herself be lessoned so, nor plainly set
Her wits to yours, forsooth, and made excuse,
—E'en then would be some stooping; and I choose
Never to stoop. Oh sir, she smiled, no doubt,
Whene'er I passed her; but who passed without
Much the same smile? This grew; I gave commands;
Then all smiles stopped together. There she stands
As if alive. Will't please you rise? We'll meet
The company below, then. I repeat,
The Count your master's known munificence
Is ample warrant that no just pretense
Of mine for dowry will be disallowed;
Though his fair daughter's self, as I avowed
At starting, is my object. Nay, we'll go
Together down, sir. Notice Neptune, though,
Taming a sea-horse, thought a rarity,
Which Claus of Innsbruck cast in bronze for me!

Approaching the Question

Read the question carefully. Look for specific words of
instruction. All too often students write good essays that

unfortunately do not answer the question and therefore do not receive high credit. The instructor is not asking you simply to toss out everything you know about the subject, but wants you to shape your information in a particular way that will prove your past learning and promote new learning as you write. Look for words such as "compare," "trace," "define," "explain," "analyze," "discuss," and so on. Do what the words tell you to do.

Exercise

Find the words of instruction in these essay questions. Explain what they are asking the student to do.

1. Explain Hopkins's view of the universe and man's place in it and demonstrate how these ideas are reflected in one of his poems.
2. Using two of the stories we have studied, discuss how they reflect situations both peculiar to their times yet universal and timeless.
3. List three of the goals of the local-color writers, and using at least two stories for illustration, argue whether or not you think they succeed.

Composing the Answer

Once you have prepared yourself and read the question carefully, you are ready to write. If you can get off to a good start and keep your wits about you, your studying will pay off. Follow the procedure outlined over the next few pages to ensure the best results.

Look for the central idea of your answer in the phrasing of the question. Notice how preliminaries in the questions in the exercises above suggest the central idea for your essay and thus begin to suggest your organization as

well. For example, an answer to the first question might
begin this way:

> Hopkins viewed the universe as
> _____ with man's place
> being _____ as reflected in
> the poem _____.

Fill in the blanks, and you have your three points to develop.

Exercise

Develop opening sentences for the questions below.
Leave blanks where you do not know the information. The
important thing here is learning how to structure opening
sentences.

1. Explain how Tennessee Williams uses symbolism in *The Glass Menagerie* to develop the character of Laura.
2. Trace Keats's use of imagery in "Ode on a Grecian Urn" to show how it leads to the philosophical assertion, "Beauty is truth, truth beauty."
3. Compare and contrast the attitude toward death in Dickinson's "Because I Could Not Stop for Death" and Dylan Thomas's "Do Not Go Gentle into That Good Night."

Get to the point immediately. You have a limited amount
of time to think and write, and your instructor's time will be
limited too. Your introduction, therefore, should involve its
reader by answering the question right away and at the
same time promising further development.

Exercise

Compare these introductory responses to the same essay
question. Which is better? Why?
Question:
Discuss the use of figurative language in Randall Jarrell's
"The Death of the Ball Turret Gunner."
Answers:

    1. Figurative language is one of the greatest
    tools of the poet. When a literal statement
    just won't do, figurative language is right

there to take on the job. There are many
forms of figurative language including. . . .
      2. Randall Jarrell's use of figurative
language, specifically metaphor, enriches his
poem, "The Death of the Ball Turret Gunner."
He intensifies the horror of this kind of
death by developing the similarities between
the death of a young man in a ball turret
and the abortion of a baby. . . .

Develop your answer with detail. Make specific references to authors and works. Refer to specific characters and incidents in the literature. Whenever possible, quote passages, or at least significant phrases, from the literature. Your essay should show that you know and appreciate the literature itself—*not* just the principles and concepts behind it. Often in an essay examination, the instructor is looking to see if you understand *how* the ideas introduced in class lectures and discussion *develop* from the poems, stories, and plays themselves.

Exercise

Read through this sample answer and mark points in it where specific information is needed. Then read through the poem in question and supply the necessary detail.
Question:
Discuss speaker in Hardy's "Channel Firing." Who is the speaker and how does his character and perspective on the situation help to develop the message of the poem?
Response:

The speaker in a poem is not always the
poet. It may be a character who makes us
like or dislike him or her. Thomas Hardy
uses a character as the speaker in "Channel
Firing." I like him and felt sorry for him
because of his predicament. He seemed very
scared and nervous about it all. I guess
Hardy made him act this way and made God
and the other characters say what they did
so we would all think seriously about
gunnery practice and what it means.

Organize logically and use key words. Your organization of paragraphs should follow standard principles of good writing. Do not push all information into a single paragraph figuring it does not matter on an essay exam. It may matter even more. Ideas are separated into paragraphs for easy, clear reading. An instructor facing 25, 50, or 100 exams needs all the help he or she can get.

Another way you can help your reader to follow you is to use key words from the question itself, especially in your topic sentences.

Exercise

Read the following question and answer. Mark key words from the question as they appear in the student's answer.
Question:
Identify the speaker and explain how the nature of what is being said and the manner of expression are typical of that character.

> "To lose one parent, Mr. Worthing, may
> be regarded as a misfortune; to lose
> both looks like carelessness."

Response:

This line is spoken by Lady Bracknell in Oscar Wilde's The Importance of Being Earnest. It is typical of her as she is arrogant in her manner and the nature of what she says is quite superficial.

It is bad enough that Lady Bracknell's manner, like others of her class and station in turn-of-the-century English society, is so arrogant. She is highly opinionated in matters ranging from food to politics and is quite judgmental in nature. She is sure that her perspective is always correct and freely points out errors in others' thought and behavior. Such is the case in this example when she casually but cruelly chastises Worthing for losing his parents as if he could help it. She acts as if she is slapping a naughty boy's hands for some social blunder.

Her arrogance is heightened by the super-
ficiality of the nature of nearly everything
she says. Not only is she smug about rebuking
Worthing for losing his parents, but she is
also blind to values deeper than the frivolous
ones of her society. She is concerned with
proprieties here as Wilde exposes what he
saw as the shallowness of the principles by
which such people governed their lives.

Avoid padding and digressions. Padding an answer on
an examination is including irrelevant material. You may
be tempted to pad in order to take up space on the page and
make your discussion look fuller. Digressing is going off on
a worthwhile topic, but not something directly germane to
the question. Padding and digressing never help in any
situation and are particularly harmful in exams. They
suggest that you don't see the point of the question or simply cannot answer it. They also take up valuable time that
you could use to show what you *do* know about the questions asked.

Exercise

Mark the following response for padding.
Question:
Discuss the use of religious imagery and symbolism in
Araby. How do these devices help us appreciate the depth
of the narrator's feelings for Mangan's sister?
Response:

Religious imagery and symbolism are found
throughout Joyce's Araby. It is set in a
Catholic neighborhood in Dublin. Religion
has always been important to Irish Catholics.
Even today the fighting continues in Northern
Ireland between Catholics and Protestants.
These people are willing to die for their
religion, which is as important to them as
it was to the boy in Araby.
He lived in a house where a priest had
died and went to a brother's school. Anyone

> who has been to parochial school knows that
> religious imagery and symbolism are a part
> of every day, as they were for this boy
> who loved Mangan's sister. . . .

And finally, remember these general rules of the game:

- Acquaint yourself with the whole exam first so that you know the various kinds of questions that appear and the value assigned to each.
- Answer the questions you feel most comfortable with first and deal with the rest later.
- Sketch a brief outline of each answer before you begin writing.
- Pace yourself so that you devote an appropriate amount of time to each question and finish in time to proofread.
- Proofread primarily for logic and coherence.
- Carry enough supplies—paper, pens, erasers, whatever—to avoid panic over the small matters.

Afterword

What is required of you in writing about literature is really no more and no less than what is required of you when you write about any other topic. You need to know your subject, have a point to make, gather concrete evidence to support your position, organize your material effectively, and demonstrate good grammar and effective style.

The purpose of this book is to remind you of these principles and to assure you that what you may have learned already about good writing applies in your literature class.

As you completed each writing assignment for your course, you may have sighed with relief and thought, "Well, that's done." But completing a paper does not really signal an end. In a way, getting your essay composed is a beginning, the wonderful kind of beginning a college education is all about—the important kind of beginning Emily Dickinson understood so well:

> A word is dead
> When it is said,
> Some say.
> I say it just
> Begins to live
> That day.